TREASURE
from
British Waters

by John Howland

RAM
BOOKS

D0332856

ISBN 0-915920-72-7
United States Library of Congress Catalog
Card No. 90-61318
Treasure from British Waters
© Copyright 1991
John Howland
Ram Publishing

First Edition Printing, April 1991

For FREE listing of related books on the use of
metal detection equipment write

Ram Publishing Co.   ●   P.O. Box 38649
Dallas, Texas 75238
U.S.A.

DEDICATION

To my wife Margaret, without whose constant goading this work would never have reached the First Draft stage.

Contents

Appendixes

About the Author

Treasure from British Waters represents a significant milestone for Ram Publishing Company. It is our first effort aimed primarily at an audience outside North America. Of course, the hobby of treasure hunting with a metal detector knows no bounds of geography. The works of Charles Garrett and Roy Lagal have universal appeal.

Still, this book is a "how-to" manual written specifically for treasure hunters who seek guidance in using metal detectors to find coins, jewelry and relics on the beaches of England and the Balearic Islands in the Mediterranean Sea. And, guidance aplenty can be found within these covers, especially for the novice beach hunter.

With more than a decade's experience using a metal detector to find treasure in Europe and the United States, John Howland lives in the Oxfordshire market town of Abingdon, some eight miles south of Oxford. When not out with a metal detector, he can usually be found following his other great passion, trout fishing, on the chalk streams and waters of Southern England. This is his first book.

Another of Great Britain's foremost metal detector hobbyists in his Foreword properly lauds the abilities of the author...his expertise, his ready wit. More importantly, John Castle points out that this book *lays the foundation, the basic rules* (for) *every beach hunter.*

So...if you plan to hunt with a metal detector in England or the Balearics, you go forearmed with this book. Yet, even if the beaches and surfs you search are on the Gulf of Mexico, Pacific shores, Spanish Main or Chesapeake Bay, you can benefit from the opinions and experiences of John Howland. Who knows? After reading *Treasure from British Waters,* you may decide to go after some of it yourself!

Hal Dawson
Editor, Ram

Dallas, Texas, U.S.A.

Foreword

I was delighted when I heard John Howland was writing a book. I was even more delighted to be asked to write this Foreword. Having known him for over a decade, I have come to respect and admire his great knowledge of treasure hunting and his determination to preserve it, at all costs. In this latter he was a powerful driving force at the British National Council for Metal Detecting, which was much the poorer when John relinquished his post as General Secretary. The American, Federation of Metal Detecting and Archaeological Clubs, Inc., was set up after John had sent many long letters across the Atlantic to Dick Stout, letters full of good advice from long experience.

John never blew his trumpet about all this, which didn't surprise me. He's not that sort of man. Rather, he just gets on with the task in hand quietly and determinedly. This perhaps is why his tasks are always done so well.

This book is another of John's tasks, executed with his usual thoroughness and good humour. Not all of you will hunt in the areas he so carefully describes...lucky those who do with this book to guide them! But everyone can learn from it. The work John has done here lays the foundation, the basic rules, which, every beach hunter should emulate if maximum success is to be obtained.

This book deserves to be a success and I'm sure it will be. There has not been a good "How-to-do-it" book (From Britain, at least) in the last fifteen years. Treasure hunters the world over will find it invaluable and enjoyable. I would hope this book is the first of many from John, a new, modern force in the long gamut of books about the greatest hobby in the world...*Treasure Hunting.*

John Castle

Aldershot, England.

Acknowledgements...

Author's Note

My sincere thanks to the following, whose help and enthusiastic assistance has been invaluable:

My father, Jack.
Dick Stout, Garland, Texas, U.S.A..
Nigel Ingram, Regton Ltd., Birmingham.
Ron Scearce, Kidlington, Oxford.
John Castle, Aldershot, Hants.
Mick & Julie Turrell, Leisure Promotions, Newbury.
Bill & Edna Irvine, Search Southwards, Bridport.
Ken Frampton, Wychwood Display Cases, Hythe, Hants.
Pat & Graham Halliday, mine hosts, "The Castle Inn," West Lulworth.
Gerald Costello, General Secretary, National Council for Metal Detecting.

Introduction

Treasure hunting is a pursuit that might well be described as the World's Second Oldest Profession! But treasure hunting with a metal detector is a very recent innovation, a product of 20th Century technology.

The development of the modern metal detector is a reflection of the huge advances made in micro-electronics. If, for example, the complex circuitry of the latest state-of-the-art metal detector were to be copied using the technology of only 30 years ago, the metal detector's control box would have to be (again, using the old "valve" systems) almost the size of a three-bedroom semi-detached house.

Today's modern treasure hunter, unlike his ancestor, is not out for a fast buck. Neither is he or she a vandal or tomb robber. Such stories are bandied about by others, particularly the small vociferous minority of ill-informed, and in some cases politically motivated, members of the once all-powerful archaeological lobby. Many of today's treasure hunters are indeed highly skilled operators of their machines. In the application and exercise of that skill individual treasure hunters have contributed enormously to the historical knowledge of this country and others.

In the decade preceding the writing of this book, there has been some 226 Treasure Trove Inquests convened, as a result of the activities of workmen, archaeologists and treasure hunters. Of these 226 Inquests, nearly 200 are the direct result of the skill of the modern treasure hunter. This record stands not only as a monument to the overall honesty and integrity of the modern treasure hunter, but to their skill in handling detectors, and to their painstaking research.

So, who are these modern treasure hunters and from whence do they come? They come in all shapes and sizes...from all walks of life...from all sections of the social spectrum

All life is well reflected within their ranks. They range from Lords to commoners, from doctors to dustmen, from the mighty to the lowly, yet they all have one thing in common ...that one special ingredient that is so sadly lacking in many aspects of today's society.

They possess that sense of camaraderie or *mateyness* that easily breaches all social barriers.

With today's modern society providing more leisure time to be enjoyed and thousands of people now taking healthy outdoor exercise whilst taking full advantage of this windfall, treasure hunting with a metal detector is an obvious choice, and one that is in harmony with the country ways. It is a pastime that is completely at home in the countryside. Yet, to the city-bound treasure hunter, it gives a greater understanding of the ways of the country and its people who have in times past, and still do, work the land.

This book then, is not so much about the ways of the countryside and its people, but of the sea. Those who choose to pursue this very specialised branch of treasure hunting popularly known as beachcombing will, I know, soon become fully absorbed in the fascinating subject.

Beachcombing has taken me to many parts of the world in which I have been able to pursue the World's Greatest Outdoor Pastime. I have indeed been fortunate.

I hope that after reading this book you too will be enthused enough to take up this exciting pastime, or, if you are already engrossed in this great hobby, that you will feel inclined to try your hand at treasure hunting in, or near the sea. If one more convert is gained, then this book will have been worth the time and effort.

John Howland

Abingdon, Oxford, England

Chapter One

Treasure hunting in the remoter parts of Britain should be an enjoyable experience. But every year too many new adventurers, involving themselves in all sorts of outdoor leisure pursuits and activities, find their enjoyment turning into a nightmare.

Every year countless thousands of visitors flock into the countryside, and…

Every year a small number return from mountains, below cliffs or from the sea in body bags.

Almost any weekend at Lulworth Cove in Dorset, despite the ample warning signs, visitors can be seen scrambling perilously close to the crumbling cliff edges. Their near-suicidal attitudes are loudly advertised by their inadequate clothing, particularly in the choice of footwear and headgear. Such ignorance or careless disregard which threatens injury or death to the thoughtless (and to those who may have to attempt their rescue) is repeated in many potentially dangerous situations, on land and water. Beachcombers confront an unusual combination of hazards...sudden storms from the sea, tidal traps, rockfalls and landslips, among the more obvious and dramatic that spring easily to mind.

It is also true that even a small accident can become a major disaster when the lone venturer is far from human help or adequate shelter. This book then, would neglect a clear duty if, while encouraging readers to the huge enjoyment and excitement to be had from modern beachcombing, it failed to hammer home the need to observe basic safety precautions.

THINK Safety

No matter what part of the coastline you intend to visit, gather as much information about the location as you can, *before* setting out on your expedition. Important information can be easily obtained from Ordnance Survey maps, and most of these are freely available in most, if not all, public libraries. You should also assemble as much further data as possible about your target zone, particularly that relating to tides and tidal ranges.

Tide information appears in the columns of "seaside" newspapers, in the weather sections of some of the "heavier" national daily papers or in special tables in tabulated form published for the information of anglers and mariners. Times of high and low tides along with the range, are the most important pieces of information you will need for both a safe and successful expedition. The tidal range reveals the distance in feet or metres that the water level rises and falls, from Dead Low Water (DLW) to Dead High Water (DHW), or vice versa.

Evidence of this range can be seen on any pier when the tide is not full. You can observe a clearly delineated black or brown mark, usually decorated with seaweed, which is formed by encrustation from floating detritus at slack water. (Something similar happens when dirty bathwater leaves evidence of the highest water level in the form of a "tide mark", though I trust the one found in your bath is not oily, black or sprouting seaweed!) The rise and fall of the tide between the tide marks on the stanchions supporting the pier or breakwater is the tidal range.

Let us suppose that you intend to visit a sandy bay surrounded by high cliffs and which you can reach only by walking along the foot of the cliffs at low tide, rounding one of the bay's "horseshoe tips." You note that the tide is ebbing and that DLW will occur in one hour. You also note that the water is now 10 metres out from the furthest point of the bay's "arms"...from this you deduce, quite correctly, that you can spend two hours, fifty minutes inside the bay before being cut off by the incoming flood tide.

It will be more difficult to estimate the depth of water at the highest point of retreat, but in this situation, and many others, it is clear that the full run of the tide is obstructed by steeply rising ground, and that the likely depth of water will be that of the full tidal range...in this hypothesis, 20 feet. If you are under, say, six feet in height and leave your retreat too late, 14 feet of that water may be of purely academic interest...*in the afterlife!*

Why two hours, fifty minutes? The timespan is calculated by noting at the time of your arrival, the position of the water's edge, and knowing from your tide tables that the tide will continue to ebb for a further one hour until DLW. Then the tide will "stand" (ie. there will be little or no tidal movement) for 50 minutes before it turns and commences to turn or flood. One hour from this moment, the water will have reached about the same position as when you first arrived.

The object of taking sensible precautions is to minimise the odds stacked *against* you;

to give you the best chance of survival if things take a turn for the worse. I always carry with me the following:

– A whistle, on string tied round my neck,
– A smoke flare. (Bought from a ship's chandlers),
– A first-aid kit.

Signaling Devices

The whistle is the kind favoured by football referees because it gives a sharp and piercing note. A smoke flare is of vital help to you and rescuers alike if you become trapped, and a helicopter is the only means of getting you to safety. The smoke released from the flare not only pinpoints your location, but shows the pilot of the helicopter the wind's speed and direction. For the pilot, this information is paramount.

My first-aid kit, a collection of plasters, antiseptic wipes, tweezers, a needle and a small tube of antiseptic cream, was cobbled together from the range of first-aid equipment sold in the Tesco superstore close to my home in Abingdon. It cost only a nominal sum.

Any reader tempted to dismiss this advice as wimpish or overcautious should bear in mind the difference between stupid bravado and bravery. There is an appropriate saying favoured by Air Force flying instructors when impressing such common sense ideas on novice pilots:

"There are old pilots and bold pilots. There are no old bold pilots!"

Chapter Two

Methodical types are more likely to read a book in the order that the author presents it, absorbing information in a sequence designed to aid comprehension and enjoyment. Less methodical readers are likely to "skip" to the heart of the matter, and then to be frustrated because they do not fully understand what they read.

When first printed in *The Searcher,* the serialised form of this book allowed no skipping forward. I have in this edition adhered to that principle, but I do promise that before long we shall be *on the beach.* Before that can happen we need to get some idea of what to expect, how to dress, what to eat, and how to prepare and use the equipment we need to be a proficient *modern beachcomber.*

All this is relevant to "success rates" in the treasure hunting hobby, whether it is enjoyed inland or on the shoreline. The most impetuous of you, like myself when I was like many other beginners, will jump in with both feet, expecting to switch on the metal detector and start hauling treasures from the ground. That is why there will always be plenty of territory for methodical, determined, experienced and SUCCESSFUL treasure hunters. So many others simply didn't start right. Or, they didn't have the luck or sheer bloody-mindedness to make up for bad preparation.

Perhaps I shall not be able to persuade you to give luck much of a helping hand. You may have already been seduced by the stories of "naturally lucky" treasure hunters, and others who hit a jackpot first time out. It would be far better for each of us to remember the comment of the top professional golfer when congratulated on his "luck" in carrying away megabucks from a particular tournament:

"Yes it's funny, the more I practice, the luckier I seem to get."

Even with skill, good research and determination there can be no guarantee of finding anything worth having on a particular day. In fact, beaches are much more fickle than other land surfaces not subject to overnight transformation by wind and water. The plough does its bit for inland treasure hunters, but this is a puny effort by comparison with the power of storms that, in a few hours, can scour many feet of sand away from productive hardpack or dump a load of barren material on the top of your happy hunting ground.

To a lesser extent, tides perform this feat daily.

While success can never be guaranteed, no planning at all is a sure recipe for failure. Apart from the major safety precautions in Chapter One, sensible attention to personal comfort will improve your enjoyment and attention level, while greatly reducing the risk of personal injury or worse. In bad conditions little precautions can make all the difference.

Planning a Trip

Let's suppose that you are planning an expedition which will last for, let's say, six hours. We will assume that you have obtained necessary information from tide tables and maps, and that you intend to make the expedition in early February. Adequate warm clothing will be needed. You will need to take along a sufficient supply of food and drink, such as sandwiches as a convenient form of nourishment. Hot tea, coffee or soup in a thermos will be welcome and beneficial. An especially welcome luxury would be a small camping stove to brew-up when you get back to the car. Fresh steaming tea at the end of the trip is a great reviver, believe me! It is also a very good idea to have a spare change of dry clothing at "base camp" just in case you are taken by surprise in a sudden squall.

If you are not carrying your thermos and "sarnies" all the way to your treasure hunting site, then you should at least take with you some high energy foods...the sort of stuff that people on diets crave and kill for: Mars bars, chocolate bars, barley sugars, mint cakes.

It also makes sense to stoke up the calories before you set out by putting a good breakfast inside you. Eggs, bacon, sausage and tomato, washed down with a couple of mugs of tea, followed by toast and marmalade, will set you up for the day. If your lunch consists of tea, six ounces of cheese, an apple and a slice of fruit cake, for example, and your pockets contain a few of the aforementioned confectionary items, you will survive the day as far as nourishment is concerned. Too many calories? Don't worry! The exercise and tough elements will soak these away.

Equipment Checks: In all this planning and packing, do not forget the main purpose of the trip, and ignore vital checks on your metal detecting equipment. The night before setting out make certain batteries have sufficient power in them, and that you are packing a spare set. Check out your head-phones to make sure they are in good working order, remembering to pack the spare set if you have one. Since you cannot do without some form of digging tool, make sure that this is packed in your haversack. Consider whether the terrain calls for optional acces-sories that should be included...perhaps small-diameter searchcoils if it's likely you'll be poking in and around rock pools (natural coin traps!).

A Final Check

Once the "hardware" is ready, make a final check on maps, tide tables, waterproof cloth-ing, first-aid kit and whistle. All should be at hand for your early morning start.

In all this there is the danger of neglecting the obvious car checks necessary before any long journey but particularly important when you are heading for the wilds. Let *WOFT* be your automotive watchword: Water, Oil, Fuel & Tyres.

This book will travel beyond the shores of Britain to sunnier climes, but in this country the months of October to April produce the most satisfactory yields from beaches. It's *quality* often...*quantity* sometimes!

So, serious beachcombers are likely to find themselves in some remote places in the depths of winter. And, some coastal regions, particularly those on the East Coast, can be bitterly cold. Those who live in the villages on "the rump" of Norfolk, for example, take a certain sadistic pride in proclaiming that their winds are lazy...*They blows through you instead of going round you, boy!* Kent's Dungeness beaches, which I frequented as a beach fisherman after the winter cod, can boast a biting, finger-numbing cold...and Northeast Scotland is not easily outclassed.

Clothing: Keeping warm and dry is not so much a case of what you wear, but more to do with HOW you wear your clothes. The long experience of mountaineers, lifeboatmen and other professionals who brave the elements, shows that the "layer" method of dressing the body is the most effective way of retaining life-saving body heat.

A suitable first layer of underclothing of the right type is essential. It could be thermal vest and pants or longjohns. Ladies tights are effective cold weather garments for both sexes. Many male outdoor types have discovered that these are comfortable and provide good value. A treasure hunting companion of mine wears them all the time, particularly since his wife found a pair on the back seat of his car!

Recommended as the next layer for the top half of the body is a thick cotton shirt...something on the lines of the sporting Tattersalls very much in vogue among the trout and salmon-angling fraternity. So too are the polo-neck shirts worn by skiers. Both types can be found in most good camping and "outdoor" shops. Marks & Spencer Ltd., are always well worth more than a cursory glance in this area, and I have no compunction at all in offering up their very high quality and robust range.

For the bottom half another more obvious unisex garment is recommended. For rugged country detecting even the ladies must wear trousers! This is simply a fact, even though there may be some difficulty in persuading them that heavyweight ex-police serge, or double thickness ex-army combat trousers which provide many extra, strong, pockets, would be "just the thing."

Denim is best left to cowboys on the range. No doubt it cuts a certain dash in the pub or disco on Saturday nights, but for our purposes it's really next to useless. Wearing soaking wet denims in a biting easterly is not an experience to be particularly recommended. Corduroy too has it's disadvantages, and my experience has been that wet corduroy takes a long time to dry out, and it's more than likely you'll be wearing it during that drying-out process.

Long-sleeved woolen sweaters are the order of the day. Wear two of "half weight" rather than just one of "full weight" because, continuing the theme of "layered dressing," two layers will be warmer than one since the trapped air provides insulation as in a cavity wall. If you have chosen to wear the polo-necked sweater rather than a conventional-style shirt, a single lambswool sweater of the type favoured by golfers will be adequate for most conditions, or you can do as I do and wear and ex-army combat sweater. Not perhaps the height of sartorial elegance, but very warm and not too restricting.

In cold weather, wind is the killer. A 20mph wind at zero degrees centigrade, for instance, has much the same effect on the human body as a drop in air temperature of at least 15 degrees C. This is what's known as "the chill factor." So, your wardrobe must include a topcoat that is windproof and, once

Treasures from the sea include valuable old jewelry and coins as well as pieces of junk, but research and practice bring success.

again, a visit to your local camping/outdoor shop should produce the appropriate garment. Be advised by the assistants, who can help you make the most of your hard-earned cash. But make sure, too, that whatever you choose has plenty of pockets.

Also be advised that anorak-style garments advertised as "windproof" are seldom waterproof. It is unlikely that you will be treasure hunting in heavy rain unless you and your machine are equally waterproof (only those metal detectors designed for immersion can be relied upon to resist damage from water seeping into the control box). But, you just might be some way from shelter or the car, when the storm breaks. Which brings us to another brand name; the PETER STORM range of polyurethane-coated nylon jackets, cagoules, and over-trousers, all wind and waterproof and able to be folded to a small yet easily stowed package.

Oxford's Ron Scearce uses a Grand Master Hunter with "discrimination" adequate for searching a beach with trash metal targets.

Footwear: Your feet are your transport, possibly over difficult terrain giving access to the site and for many miles in a long day's treasure hunting. They need special attention. Most fell-walkers and ramblers prefer to wear two pairs of socks and for two very good reasons: warmth and the prevention of blisters. Ideally, you should have a thin pair worn next to the skin, with a thick pair of woolen "sea-boot" types worn over these. Avoid wearing darned socks because these are likely to produce painful blisters....hence the expression, one supposes..."darned socks!"

Many styles of boot and walking shoe may be appropriate, but rule out everyday office shoes, casuals and trainers, especially in winter. A stout pair of conventional walking boots, or the padded Wellington type sold under the name DERRYBOOT, for example, will serve you well. Ordinary non-padded Wellingtons will soon make your feet cold, unless you do as I do and wear slip-on foot insulators. But, these non-padded boots, generally loose fitting and sometimes abrasively lined, will be uncomfortable over any distance.

When buying boots of any sort it is advisable to wear the socks of the type you intend to wear on-site. Then, when you try on the boots, you can make sure that your heel does not ride up inside the heel of the boot--a short cut to blisters--and that the right balance exists between giving your toes adequate space, but not so much room that your feet slide forward, encouraging sore toes and blisters. This can happen during a long descent to the beach as the weight of your body slides your toes forward.

About Sandals...

Avoid wearing sandals if you are likely to be searching in, over and under rocks or in rockpools. Sandals simply do not give your ankles the necessary support, and are little protection against broken glass or jagged rock. Lightweight boots or heavy-duty trainers are more suitable warm-weather footwear. You may not look too elegant, but remember...yours are the feet and ankles at risk.

At the other extremity we find our neck and head, the thermostat of the body, through which 50% of all body heat is lost. A simple operation on a woolly bobble hat can provide suitable headgear. The bobble must go because it gets in the way of headphones. For really cold weather a balaclava is unequaled.

Your choice of gloves will have a lot more

to do with personal notions of comfort and protection, and the type of metal detector you use…whether precise adjustments of finger controls are often required, for example, and whether you are particularly concerned to protect the fingers from dirt or cuts as well as the cold.

Mitts of the sort with no finger cover are a compromise between warmth and precision while the more capacious over-mitten, with one compartment for all fingers and another for thumb, may be a comfort if anchored by a cord and easily slipped off.

The very latest development in sports gloves comes from America, a development that maximises the qualities of neoprene. Although the gloves are intended for use by anglers who need to make continual fine adjustments to the drag controls of their fixed-spool reels, they might well prove to be the ideal type of winter glove for all treasure hunters. They are, I'm told, fairly expensive.

In Britain, and particularly when talking about coastal areas, it is not sensible to make broad distinctions between summer and winter climate extremes. You can probably imagine a cold, wet and windy day on the beach in August and a balmy sunny day in winter when it might be possible, or even essential for comfort, to search in shirt sleeves. Spare clothes and open options are always advisable.

Assuming that you can count on a warm day, light summer gear may well be the most comfortable, though such are the extremes of our "temperate" climate, sunburn is another hazard to be taken very seriously. This is particularly true when sea breezes and water reflections disguise and exaggerate the drying and burning effects of the sun.

For such reasons lightweight trousers are a more versatile garment than shorts. A baseball-type cap, Polaroid sunglasses and some protection for the back of the neck are the front line defences against the worst the sun can do. Don't take your shirt off if you are a recent arrival on a Mediterranean summer site. A *maximum* of 30 minutes skin exposure on day one, increasing by 15 minutes a day, will probably give you a nice tan without burning or sunstroke. But, err on the side of caution.

A final word on summer wear concerns your hands. Gloves obviously will not be necessary for protection against the weather. But, broken glass, jagged metal or cut tinplate, and a few other hazards not yet specified, will suffice to justify the admonition never to search in sand with fingers to recover objects pinpointed with your metal detector. That's what your trowel and sandscoop are for...among the accessories to be looked at in the next chapter.

Chapter Three

A final look at accessories assembled for your first beach trip will bring us, at last, to the metal detector itself. But, you will also need a carrier for spare clothes, sustenance, first-aid kit, etc. I favour a haversack of the sort similar to airline shoulder bags or a fisherman's bag with a good strong wide shoulder strap. Ideally, you will need something of about 14x12x5 inches, a carrier that is at least large enough to contain a thermos flask in addition to eats, first-aid kit, maps, small towel or handwipe, digging aids, and spares (screwdriver, batteries, perhaps a spare set of lightweight headphones) and safety equipment.

The first-aid kit might well include insect repellent and cream to soothe insect bites and stings...not a minor consideration if you are treasure hunting abroad. Should you be unfortunate enough to have a run-in with the white-faced hornet or the Mediterranean

31

scorpion, the pain of the encounter may convince you that you should have packed a .38 Smith & Wesson to deaden the pain! Remember this when tempted to poke about with fingers in rock cracks, holes or other places into which you cannot see. You'll only make the mistake once! There are special-purpose tools for digging, probing and sandscooping. Use them!

It is also worthwhile carrying a pocket-knife, bottle opener and whistle (better still if the whistle is worn round the neck). You should know that the international distress signal is six whistle blasts blown in quick succession, repeated after one minute. If you hear such a signal, reply with three blasts, followed by three more after a minute's interval. Then, keep repeating the blasts until you have made visual contact with the person in trouble.

The basic tool for digging and recovery is a trowel...not the sort used for gardening, they are far too fragile...but a purpose-built digger made of hard-wearing stainless steel. It will not come cheap, but it will withstand the punishment and rigours that treasure hunting inflicts on digging tools. One of the very best in my opinion is the Leisure Trowel supplied by Regton Ltd. of Birmingham. The

American 'Alligator' trowel, perhaps best suited to the needs of the inland treasure hunter is also worth considering. These have to be purchased by mail-order from the United States. Both trowels are virtually indestructible. A set of bicycle-tyre levers is useful for prising objects out of cracks and rock fissures.

Using a Sandscoop

In soft, dry sand where the digging is easy you may favour a sandscoop...a combined sieve and shovel sometimes made of sturdy plastic. Metal is stronger of course, but the plastic scoop will not give your detector any misleading signals. It is a simple matter to sift away dry sand before picking out the ancient gold coin that is left behind.

You need somewhere to store your newly found gold coins and other recovered items as you move along the beach. For example a proper "finds apron"--something like a carpenter's nail apron--or a belt-slung side-bag. That latter is my preference: supplied as an optional extra from the manufacturer of my metal detecting equipment, Garrett.

Metal detectors come in a wide variety of styles, shapes, colours and price. Yet, none of these clearly observed differences provide any indication of which machine is right for you! Whether you spend a thousand pounds or fifty pounds you can expect to own a machine that will give a clear, unmistakable signal when a metal item is within detection range. They will all perform the basic function which, when the hobby first began, many dismissed as an impossibility, some sort of elaborate confidence trick.

In general, cheaper models will not have the performance capabilities of more expensive ones. It is the sort of choice that faces the car buyer. The now defunct Ford Cortina, for example, was a very popular and reliable family saloon sold at a very competitive price. Compare the old Cortina with the AC Cobra costing ten times as much. Both cars have four wheels and an engine, but the Cobra is the high-performance car. Still, in certain traffic conditions the Cobra would take the same time as the Cortina to complete its journey. The point of this analogy is to emphasise that choosing the right type of metal detector for the type of searching you intend to do will make a greater contribution to your success and enjoyment than simply spending the most you can afford.

Some metal detectors turn in a better performance on the beach than others designed to locate more deeply buried objects on land.

Searching on beaches and coastal areas requires a metal detector that can discriminate against (cut out or identify signals from) the tons of silver foil, bottle tops, ring-pulls and all the other metallic trash that is left behind on popular beaches everywhere.

Offer a Compromise

There are detectors that excel in such qualities but which, as in many other areas of high-tech manufacture, offer a particular compromise in the mix of desirable options. It is often true that the strengthening of one quality makes another difficult to achieve.

Like all other types of detector, discriminators emit an electromagnetic field from the searchcoil. When the coil is passed over a hidden metal object, even though buried, the magnetic field is disturbed. Through a complicated series of electronic phases, the internal circuitry of the detector measures the conductivity of the metal object and converts this information into recognised signals, sound and/or visual (meter reading).

These permit the operator to identify whether or not a particular signal is worth digging. What a discriminator will not do, despite the legends on some meters, is to positively distinguish between a coin and a ring, for example, and all other objects.

The indications on a meter are not fraudulent. They are a genuine attempt to show the likely points at which there is the best chance that the signal is connected with a ring or a coin, or even a coin of a particular denomination. This is useful additional and simplified information, particularly for beginners. More experienced users, particularly if they have been operating one machine for a long time, will notice many other subtle variations in its signals. By associating every signal with those related to previous finds, they learn far more from a meter than simply what it is expected to do.

The essential point about discriminator-type machines is that they are built to help the searcher decide whether or not digging is likely to be worthwhile, or to eliminate altogether some signals from "unwanted" metals.

So, we have gone some way towards answering, or at least sensibly refusing to answer, the usual first question asked by beginners to the pastime, *"What's the best detector to buy?"* The more you pay for a detector, the more sophisticated features you can expect to find. Plus, there is likely to be a connection between higher prices and greater depth capabilities. The limit of the most expensive machines is likely to be ten to twelve inches for a coin-sized objects while machines with a purchase price well into the lower bands of the pricing scales, may well be defeated at two to three inches.

How Deep?

Which is the subject of the next-most asked question: "*How deep do they find things?*" Depth depends on a number of factors not restricted to the detector's price and method of working.

Size of the target is very important: in general the larger the object, the deeper it can be located. The length of time an object has been in the ground is also an important factor. This relates to size of object because there is a leaching effect of metallic elements from long-buried objects which enlarges the "signaling area," of say, a coin.

Other factors affecting possible depth of recovery are:

● Size (or diameter) of the searchcoil,

● Power output of the metal detector,

● Angle in relation to the searchcoil at which the target lies,

●Mineralisation of the surrounding ground,

● Type of metal from which the object is made,

- Electromagnetic frequency emitted by the detector, and
- Finally, but most controllable, the sensitivity setting of the machine.

There is no maximum setting suitable to all ground conditions, and it follows that adjustable detectors will be more versatile by allowing maximum setting where ground conditions allow it. The ability of an operator to analyse ground conditions and to set the controls of a detector to achieve optimum performance cannot be bought over the counter as one might with a much sought-after accessory. Experience will tell the operator what searchcoil to choose to benefit most different operating characteristics. The permutations of detectors, interchangeable searchcoils and operating settings are almost endless. The best results are probably obtained consistently by those people who have long experience with a particular, good machine, in addition to experience, memory and acquired instinctive reactions to signals from objects of all descriptions in all types of ground conditions.

Whilst the discriminator is probably the most popular and widely used type of detector for our purposes, machines that work on the pulse induction principle deserve a special mention in the context of beachcombing. Such machines rapidly "pulse" an electronic signal into the ground many times per second. Their principal asset is exceptional depth capability, while their principal drawback is a bias towards iron. At the same time they are reasonably good at rejecting silver foil (if not better at this than some discriminators)...altogether a formidable combination on beaches where, generally, there is little iron.

On mud flats, or areas of sand that are uncovered by the ebb tide, these machines are preeminent. Gradually manufacturers are reducing problems of weight and high battery drain, and it seems likely continued research and development will hold the key to the door through which many others will follow.

Metal detectors derive their power from dry cell or dry cell rechargeable batteries, such as the penlight AA types that power small torches and portable radios. It can take six or eight of these to produce a total of 9 or 12 volts. Some manufacturers opt to use 9v PP3 batteries. Generally, you can expect to obtain 15 to 20 hours of useful life from a set of disposable batteries, while the rechargeables will more likely expire after about 8 hours.

In return for a larger capital investment, dry cell rechargeables are cheaper, if not so convenient, to use over the long term. They also have a nasty tendency to expire without warning when their time is up. In accordance with a well known law, this will happen when you least want it to happen. If you choose such a power system, it is a sensible precaution to always carry a spare set, fully charged, or, where it is an option, to have immediate access to conventional dry cell types.

Maintaining optimum performance from your detector also depends on recognising that it is not a toy but a sensitive piece of electronic equipment which, looked after well, will give many years of good service.

DON'T poke about inside it with a screwdriver; spray any chemicals inside or outside; expose it to harmful dust or extremes of temperature; leave it in your car on a hot day or subject it to any extremes of hot or cold weather for a lengthy period.

DO read the instruction manual before all else. After every outing be sure to wipe down

This handsome Victorian silver Vesta box was found by a beach hunter's metal detector. A closer inspection shows its hallmarks.

your detector with a damp cloth; try to keep the control box protected with a plastic cover (there are commercial options, or you can make one yourself); transport your detector from place to place with care (there are carry bags on the market).

Even if all seems well, it's sensible to get your machine back to the manufacturer or importer every two years or so for a retune and general "once over." A searchcoil cover is a worthwhile investment, particularly when the machine is brand new. The coil takes most of the inevitable knocks and scratches in use, and only a fool would pay good money for a second-hand machine with a search head that looks as though it had been used for driving in six-inch nails. Because the alignment of windings in the coil is vital to the performance of the detector, searchcoil heads deserve to be treated with great respect.

Above: Before searching any beach, make certain you are aware of all local regulations as well as tide levels that can be expected.

Below: Discrimination controls, at left, on this Garrett AT4 Beach Hunter have been dialed to settings suitable for most beaches.

If you have never used a metal detector before, I'll wager that your interest was first aroused by watching, or talking to, some treasure hunter in action on a popular beach. And, you were probably struck immediately by the idea that the most curious thing about this odd-ball character was that while everyone else was soaking up sun, the person with the metal detector was wearing headphones!

These are important items of equipment, even though most detectors have a loudspeaker system that can allow you to operate without headphones. They are not an expensive item and the advantages of headphones are many:

● Because they concentrate your aural attention on the smallest and faintest of sounds, you can detect smaller and deeper targets.

● Because they use less power, they help to extend the life of the detector's batteries.

● They block out background noise such as pounding waves.

● As an added bonus, will keep your ears warm on cold and windy days.

Some manufacturers supply headphones along with the detector, others don't, though it's quite likely that if you have just spent a couple of hundred pounds on a machine the supplier, if he's any good, will throw in a pair, gratis, as a goodwill gesture. In any case a good and appropriate main or reserve pair of headphones from a metal detecting supplier will cost only a few pounds.

Chapter Four

Now that you have your detecting equipment, what will you do with it? For the moment try to imagine that it is a warm, sunny day and that you are on a sandy beach, armed with your new detector, headphones set at a jaunty angle, with spade or trowel at the ready. You have high expectations.

You will begin at the top end of the beach, a spot favoured by holidaymakers and day-trippers, where it is likely there will be a few modern coins lying about for you to cut your teeth on. Shrewdly assessing the likelihood that there will also be plenty of junk lying hereabouts, particularly silver paper, you set the machine's discrimination control to **MAX.** and proceed to search the area.

WRONG!

As with other fine sounding controls-- "sensitivity" for example--you can have too much of a good thing. Let us suppose you had also remembered to switch **ON** the detector, yet you had spent 15 minutes of fruitless searching. Now is the time to think more carefully about how you should use the discrimination control…to think again about what it is capable of doing and what are the best, and common sense, ways of using it.

The purpose of the discrimination control is to wipe out signals from various types of material that the detector would be able to recognise with the control set to its minimal setting, usually, **0** on a numbered scale up to **10**. Since the discrimination setting relates to electromagnetic properties of various metals, not their value or collector's interest, there is always the probability of writing off some "good stuff" along with the "bad." Here it is taken for granted that you are not eager to spend time digging silver foil. Well, at maximum setting of the discrimination control you have solved that particular problem with a vengeance. Your method is marginally better than not switching on the detector at all (assuming that you don't mind wasting the batteries and that you did want to find that oil drum!)

Time will be better spent looking in detail at our discrimination chart. Run your finger along the row of numbers at the base until you reach **6**. Now move your finger upwards until you come to the magic words, "gold ring." The message is that you might find a chunky gold ring at this setting and, looking to the right, you see that ring pulls, 50p pieces, old pennies and oil drums are all still within your grasp. If you look to the left you will see that, sure enough, silver foil has been wiped out, but so have thin-section gold rings, 5p coins, 10p coins and all other ancient coins, brooches, pendants, tokens, etc, that happen to fall into this broad band also. The message is writ large on this chart as a permanent reminder:

"The higher the setting the more you LOSE...bad and good.

It follows that the greater the variety and volume of junk on any particular site, the higher is the discrimination level you may be forced to use. It also follows that some sites will have such a high ratio and variety of junk to desirable finds that they are just not worth searching.

Think about this carefully and you will begin to see that a little workstudy must go into deciding where to search and which discrimination level to use. To take a ridiculous example, would you be prepared to dig four gold rings for every ring pull, or, say, six ancient silver coins for every piece of folded silver foil? The more likely ratios call for more subtle judgments, but the principle holds good: *assessing how much junk is acceptable for the occasional worthwhile find.*

Just how would you set about deciding that, on a new site? Back to the beach. It is virtually certain that so far, in the peak traffic area of the beach you have been working, you will have rejected some coins, and any gold ring that just might have been under the searchcoil. And you might not have learned anything about how junky the site might be...you've simply guessed at it.

So this time, set the discrimination control to **0** (zero). That means you will pick up signals from all metallic objects that the detector is capable of recognising. Working at that setting you will soon have a pretty clear idea about just how much junk and what sort of junk is hidden in the sand.

Perhaps after five minutes you have a bagful of silver foil. Crank the discrimination control up to the **2** setting and notice the effect. No more silver foil, or perhaps only much-folded pieces? Well, that's good! You have eliminated the major problem and you will not have rejected too much more. But it would be typical of this situation that you will continue to dig ring-pulls, perhaps a plague of them. This is the most hated trash in the world of treasure hunting not just because ring-pulls seem to be everywhere, but also because they sit high up in the discrimination band, and awfully close to much more desirable finds.

The '2' Setting

At your **2** setting you can be happy in the knowledge that 5p pieces, 10p pieces, gold rings, 50p pieces and oil drums will all register. But now comes the real test to see whether you might make a proficient "modern beachcomber." You have recovered your umpteenth ring-pull, each time responding to a good, strong, sharp signal that might just have been a coin or ring. What do you do?

If you set the discrimination level to **7**, you will avoid ring-pulls but there are also many desirable items "out of range." Only items higher that **7** on the chart will be accessible. The next oil drum just might be full of gold coins, but is that probability enough to keep you going? True, 50p coins are still in reach, but it's not likely there will be an abundance of these. And, the only old pennies worth having are 1933 vintage which are all accounted for!

You opt for putting up with digging ring-pulls, and that decision earns you many points towards your beachcombing proficiency badge. But don't get too big-headed....someone, somewhere inland, has blistered palms from digging ring-pulls from 8-inches down in hard ground. Your soft dry sand should have made the decision pretty easy!

The discrimination chart is exact enough for our purposes, but it is a composite presentation of basic discriminating machines, not any one particular make or model. The latest discriminators do not have a single cut-off point below which everything else is lost. The ring-pull problem, for example can be much reduced by *Notch* discriminators which allow a narrow band of rejection while signals on either side in the spectrum can be accepted. Garrett Electronics has now taken the principle of notch discrimination a stage further with what they term *Dual Discrimination*, whereby the entire length of the electromagnetic conductivity spectrum is split into two clearly defined groups: ferrous and non-ferrous. The metal detectors illustrated in many of the photographs accompanying this book, the Garrett AT4, and the Garrett Grand Master Hunter CX II have this advanced system of discrimination.

Another problem is that the higher discrimination is set, the less depth will be obtained. *All is compromise.* At the top end of the beach where we have begun our practical lesson, high levels of junk may mean that your compromise between not missing anything, and sensible "workstudied" detecting will mean relatively high discrimination setting. But further down the beach, following a retreating tide over wet sand, a reassessment of junk levels may show there is little trash about. In these circumstances I would keep the **Discrim** to a bare minimum, and dig all signals. Experience shows that there is relatively little trash below the high water mark, but this is the area where items of gold jewellery can be expected, with much of it, (thin section gold rings set with precious stones) falling into the lower end of the discrimination scale.

The sensitivity control is another fine-sounding adjustment that should be treated with extreme caution. It may help sensible use of this device if you think of it as an anti-sensitivity control. In all but perfect conditions, the detector is likely to be virtually useless when set to maximum sensitivity. In many conditions it may need to be set well short of that for optimum performance. When you are starting out, I recommend that you keep this control set at minimum until you have become familiar with all other aspects of operating your machine.

With the sensitivity control set too high for the prevailing ground conditions, or if set to maximum, the detector will become super-sensitive. It will pick up all sorts of useless mineral information causing a constant crackling in the headphones masking out the more positive signals you want to hear. Backing off the control effectively makes the detector more stable, and increases your finds rate. It may help if you think about driving in fog (when conditions are far from perfect) and remember the difference between using dipped headlights and main beam. The reduced power is more effective...you can see further with dipped headlights than the more powerful main beam.

Turning down the power of your detector, as it were, often gives you more usable depth. Garrett Electronics, uniquely, have renamed this control on their detectors as a **Depth Control,** a description more accurate perhaps than "sensitivity control." But, the one constant complaint I have about detector manufacturers advertising is the oft heard claim that machine X or Y is "more sensitive" or "has more sensitivity." What they ought to be saying is that our machine has a sensitivity control that can almost switch it off! The first manufacturer to achieve this will be well along the road to giving pro and semi-pro treasure hunters a much-needed requirement.

Inevitably, the advice in this chapter is generalised. It will help you to understand any machine and the Owner's Manual that accompanies it. But that particular publication must be read, reread and read again. You should give extra special attention to setting-up instructions and follow exactly that section dealing with the tuning of the detector to its "threshold" point. This is a simple operation on most detectors, but if care is not taken in the overall operation, or perhaps that special sequence in which tuning to "threshold" is first achieved, your detector will not perform to its full potential.

Reading the Beach

"The tide comes in, and the tides goes out. Another day, another dollar."

How different will be the meaning of those words to a man bored with his daily toil, and another watching the beach for golden opportunities to enjoy his hobby. For beachcombers ancient and modern it is a matter of great importance that the tide goes in and out, and more so that waves crash upon the beach. Every tide that comes and goes changes the physical state of the beach. If you are patient, the power of the sea can be made to work for you.

"You can't fight the sea, only make friends with it" is an old adage that I first heard many years before beachcombing with a metal detector was even dreamed of. Then I was content messing about in boats, but the truth of the saying was just as clear.

An ability to understand the moods and natural actions of the sea will be of enormous help to you. Ignore what the sea is telling, and you will not be a successful treasure hunter.

Disregarding the freak-effects of certain coastal geography, there are two full tides in something just over 24 hours. The incoming tide, the flood tide, is on the move for six hours, and the outgoing tide, the ebb tide, for another six. But at "high" and "low" waters, the tidal movement is nil, and the tide "stands" for about 50 minutes, before moving "in" or "out." The moon, not the sun, controls the tides.

At the full and new phases of the moon the gravitational pull of the moon on the earth is greatest and creates the largest tidal movements--the spring tides--when water comes farther up the beach at high tide and goes out farther at low tide. Between spring tides, when the gravitational pull is less and the range of water movement is less, is the period of the neap tides.

The combination of a storm and a high spring tide is a powerful engine to erode the beach. Free of chargē, the sea will do much more for you than a mechanical digger could in the same time. You will have new territory to search...the effect is of having a huge increase in detection depth, without having far to dig: sand and pebbles have been scoured away from above deeply buried, long-lost coins and artifacts.

Prime Time Tides

Each year there are exceptionally large tidal ranges at the times of the spring and autumn equinoxes. These tides have often produced bonanzas and are well-known as "prime time" by experienced beachcombers. In remoter areas it is quite likely at these seasons that a treasure hunter using sophisticated metal detection equipment over certain areas of beach and foreshores, will be searching areas that have never before been searched in this way. These places, it should be remembered, have been trapping metallic evidence of history for thousands of years. Thus, prospects become very exciting indeed.

Tidal Drift.

Tidal, or longshore, drift is the general and consistent direction of the tidal flow along the coastline. On the East Coast of Britain, the drift is north to south. On the South Coast it is east to west. On the West Coast it is south to north. That is the overall pattern sometimes interrupted by unusual local conditions, particularly around headlands, where the flow could be reversed.

Longshore drift moves with it sand, shingle and pebbles. It threatens to strip some beaches of fine sand which is so popular with visitors. To counteract this erosion and continue attracting the tourist trade, local authorities build a series of groynes running up the beach from the sea. Many stretches of coastline are, thus, neatly *boxed*...and many coins and other items that we hope to find are neatly filed away!

Close observation of the "boxes" will show that sand and shingle is piled much higher on one side than the other...always higher on the

Always search near groynes such as these at Christchurch Beach, Hants., which help to retard beach erosion but also "file" and "box" treasures such as the silver coin of Henry VIII, shown at bottom.

side of the groyne that opposes the longshore drift. Both sides are worth searching because where material is piled high, there will also be coins, jewellery and other artifacts that have been moved along with the sand and shingle. On the other side, where the longshore drift has renewed its efforts, much of the covering top sand has been shifted away from deeper, denser layers so that older losses may have been brought within reach of your detector. Both sides of the groynes should be searched.

Influence of the Waves

Waves don't usually roll straight up the beach to break and then retreat along the same line. What really happens is the waves hit the beach at an angle, let's say 45 degrees, to the waterline of the beach, but recede at right angles to this waterline. Consequently any object being moved by the waves will be washed in at a 45-degree angle then down again at 90 degrees, each time being shifted in the direction of the longshore drift along a zig-zagging route.

A Beach Hunter AT4 is used to search a natural coin trap such as the groynes shown here and on the opposite page.

Thus, such objects move laterally along the beach and it is not uncommon to discover many coins in one particular spot. The power of the receding (broken) waves slowly diminishes as they roll backwards, losing their "grip" on objects...the most dense or heavier objects being the first to break free, the lighter ones later. This is an automatic grading process that has some interesting effects for beachcombers. For example, coins of a similar denomination, because they are a similar size and weight, will be deposited in lines parallel with the waterline. Of course, there will be some mixing, but on a prolific beach the division may be very clear. Obviously it make sense to adapt your search patterns to this. I have made a handsome profit on a little bay in the Channel Islands by following the "50p line."

Before closing this chapter I want to lay to rest one of the greatest and most often repeated misunderstandings connected with beachcombing with a metal detector. Other than in this book, you will come across the phrase *Salt-wet sand.* Exactly what this phrase means I'm not quite sure. What I suspect it means is *Sand, wetted with salt water.* Some will tell you that salt, when wet, affects the performance of a metal detector in the same way as mineralised ground. Nonsense! Take no notice whatsoever. But, sand that has been doused with sea water is mineralised, does affect the performance of a metal detector, but has nothing to do with *salt!*

Sea water, apart from the salt it contains, has dissolved in it, many minerals including gold and silver. It is these minerals, not the salt nor the sand, that can affect your detector. Thus, whenever you are searching over sand, particularly sand exposed to sea water, always turn down the sensitivity settings of the detector so as to make the detector "blind" to these minerals. Equally, when hunting over wet sand, these minerals can be "tuned out" by careful use of the discrimination control.

To do this, first tune the detector to its threshold point with the searchcoil held well away from the ground. Then lower the coil to the wet sand. If there is an increase in the audio pitch, raise the coil, set the discrimination or sensitivity higher and lower the coil to the sand. Keep doing this until the correct setting is achieved which will be when there is little or no increase in the detector's audio tone.

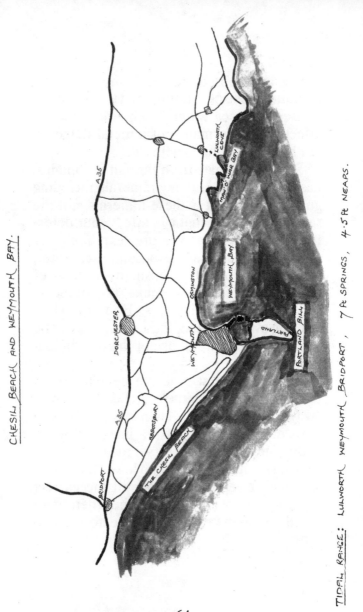

CHESIL BEACH AND WEYMOUTH BAY.

BRIDPORT

A 35

ABBOTSBURY

THE CHESIL BEACH

DORCHESTER

A 35

WEYMOUTH

OSMINGTON

WEYMOUTH BAY

PORTLAND

PORTLAND BILL

MAN O' WAR BAY

LULWORTH COVE

TIDAL RANGE: LULWORTH WEYMOUTH BRIDPORT, 7 Ft SPRINGS, 4.5 Ft NEAPS.

64

Chapter Five

In the ensuing chapters I shall deal with some of my favourite beachcombing locations...places where, with my help, you too can experience the sheer thrill and excitement of modern beachcombing. Their order of presentation need not be construed as any order of preference, productivity or anything else. It simply represents the order in which I chose to commit my thoughts and observations to paper. To begin we shall look at...

Dorset Beaches

The coastline of Dorset stretches from Poole Harbour in the east to the pleasant town of Lyme Regis in the west, along which the visitor will view some of the most impressive and awe-inspiring natural beauty to be found anywhere in the British Isles. It is a coastline too of considerable interest to the beachcomber.

In whatever coastal village you choose to halt your ramblings you will encounter tales of smugglers, pirates, wreckers and shipwrecks. It is a coastline which also was favoured by invaders throughout our history with the Romans, Saxons and Vikings in particular leaving much evidence behind of their presence. The sea still surrenders intriguing samples from ancient shipwrecks, sometimes in the form of gold and silver coins and ingots. In this chapter we will pinpoint those areas that will repay careful searching.

Lulworth Cove and Man O' War Bay

Lulworth Cove is a popular anchorage and haven for small boats, as it has always been. Almost a complete circle about a quarter of a mile in diameter carved from the surrounding chalk cliffs, its perfection makes it a spectacular attraction for day-trippers. Sheltered from rough water in northerly winds, it can become a graveyard for any vessel caught in the cove by a sudden shift in the wind to the south or southwest. The cove is wide enough at its entrance to allow the passage of fairly large ships and deep enough (mean average: 12 feet) to prevent all but the largest vessels from grounding.

Lulworth Cove is a veritable treasure house of folk lore with tales of smugglers, piracy, ghostly apparitions, headless coachmen and the phantom Roman army of

Bindon Hill. The latter refers to an army of Legionnaires which marches along Bindon Hill to its camp on Ring's Hill. The thud of their horses hooves and of the men themselves is, witnesses testify, plainly heard. On the nights when the "army" marches no rabbits run and no dogs go near. But perhaps Lulworth's most celebrated "day-tripper" is thought to have been Napoleon Bonaparte.

The Napoleon Tale

I am going to relate this incident simply for the sake of interest. I found it most intriguing, and I'm sure you will too: A local farmer had married the daughter of a china manufacturer, and the young lady being of good breeding had been taught French, which at the close of the 18th Century was a less than usual accomplishment. She had been taught French, at some expense to her father, because in his china clay dealings with the Sevres potteries he needed someone who could handle correspondence and related business matters.

The young lady's husband, a farmer of local repute and from good yeoman stock, could not refrain from a little smuggling now and again and was something of a leading light in the business of illicit gin, brandy and tobacco trading. It seems that on one particular night her husband and his companions were doing a "run," and she feared greatly for his safety...for the press-gangs were abroad looking for "volunteers" to join the Royal Navy, as were the smuggler's arch-rivals, the Excise men.

Leaving her farmhouse at St. Andrews, she ran down the road to the Cove in a state of panic for she had seen a strange ship lying-to at anchor close to the Cove and feared that it could be either the press-gang or the Revenue Cutter. As she reached the Cove she saw a longboat coming ashore in the moonlight. She had just time to hide behind some rocks as the keel of the longboat grated on the shingle gravel beach. Two men leaped ashore.

Familiar with the appearance of Napoleon, she recognized to her horror in the light of a lantern, that one of the men was, indeed, the Young Emperor himself! Understanding their conversation (in French) she could hear them discussing the possibility of landing an invasion force along this piece of coastline. The two men pored for some time over a map and talked heatedly. Finally, Napoleon shrugged his shoulders with a regretful *Impossible,* and the pair departed the Cove and rowed back to their ship. The frigate slipped anchor and in broad moon-light made off to France. What might have been Lulworth Cove's place in history had it not been for Napoleon's *Impossible,* one can only wonder.

The lady was born in 1784 and died in 1888 and told her story to a Miss Loader of Lul-worth, in person, who sensibly made a record, subsequently published but not widely so, in 1932.

Back to beachcombing. Nowadays the Cove is swamped by tourists in summer and the cafe, pub and coffee shop owners do a roaring trade. In winter months it is a very different tale with most of these estab-lishments closed and the outdoor population reduced to a few hardy inshore fishermen.

October through to April are the months that interest us. Autumn and winter storms will be working for the beachcomber tearing back covers of shingle to expose the underly-ing chalk, taking us closer to the multitude of coins and artifacts deposited over the years.

Driving down the fairly steep hill on the approach road you will pass through the ham-let of West Lulworth where on your right hand side, you will see the Castle Inn, a thatched building some 450 years old. The Castle Inn serves some of the finest ales to be had for many miles around, along with an unrivaled selection of hot and cold food. The Castle's accommodation is quite superb and reasonably priced. The warm and friendly atmosphere of the beamed bars make the Castle a considerable attraction after a long, cold and windy day's treasure hunting in the Cove. Indeed, it is quite a superb base for a winter weekend's beachcombing.

Continuing along the road through the village will eventually bring you to a large car park on the right hand side, a short step to the Cove itself. Car parking is free in the winter months, or was at the time of writing.

Leaving the car park on foot for about 200 yards down the narrow lane will bring you to the Cove itself, and, if you've got things right, the tide will be about two hours from DLW. If the tide is "in," you might just as well spend your time back at the Castle Inn because you can forget about searching hereabouts at High Water...there just isn't any beach!

Looking across the Cove to your left you will (or should, if you have done your calculations correctly) see a large chalk boulder that is almost fully exposed by the ebb tide. Head for this boulder which is visible in the photo on Page 77 just above the bow of the boat marked 723. Use it as your westerly marker.

Your marker to the east will be the fresh-water "stream" that trickles across the sand and shingle some 200 yards east of the boulder. Between these two markers is where you will hunt.

Curiously, it is the *offshore* gales that strip this beach of shingle so if your journey is in the wake of northwesterly or northeasterly gale with readings well up in the Beaufort Scale (7's or higher), conditions will be promising. When overlying shingle is reduced to its minimum, the chalk base will be visible. Hidden in cracks and fissures of this chalk is a treasure trove of old coins, rings and all imaginable trinkets. I know of fifteen gold coins of French and Portuguese origin that have been recovered from this area in recent years. Five of these were found on two consecutive visits to the Cove by one lucky hunter. They were of course, properly declared to the Receiver of Wreck, and later returned to the finder.

Do not ignore the base of the cliffs...coins and rings can be, and are, thrown there by the action of the waves. Other parts of the Cove, beyond the suggested markers, will also produce coins, but the prime territory is as specified. The western end of the bay is full of junk, including innumerable ring-pulls. I have no doubt that this end must also contain "collectables," but battling through a carpet of aluminum junk in the past has drained any enthusiasm of mine, for this part of the Cove.

On this scouting expedition we shall return to the car park for a brew-up and consider the next promising territory, Man O' War Bay.

Leaving the car park where it is, you'll be faced with a fairly steep climb up the tarmac-surfaced path to a stile where you can reward yourself by getting back your breath…and losing it again when you focus on the view. Climbing the stile, follow the path down to the shingle and sand beach, our destination…

Man O' War Bay.

You should not plan to work both ter-ritories on the same day for, once again, you want the tide on ebb with two hours to DLW to make the most of both areas, and you can't be in two places at once! All along Man O' War beach right up to the stunning lagoon at the western end and around the western point gold coins have been found akin to those retrieved from Lulworth Cove. I have spent many a pleasant hour here in the company of John Castle, one of Britain's top-gun THers. a master of his craft and a sturdy, resolute defender of the treasure hunting hobby.

The lagoon at the western end of the beach will handsomely repay anyone prepared to work about six feet out from the shoreline with a fully submersible metal detector. Here, there must be a wealth of material for those prepared to cross over into the "New Frontier" of treasure hunting, which requires a wet suit and other specialized paraphernalia. Caution and common sense is also required, as well as a very specialised metal detector similar to Garrett Electronic's AT4 (All Terrain) submersible. I now use an AT4 for *all* my beachcombing activities, having updated from the AT3 which has accounted for many coins and trinkets recovered from Mediterranean beaches.

We must hurry back to the car; there may be time for a bite to eat, but there is more to see in the immediate area as we move west to...

Osmington

Driving from the car park back towards West Lulworth, turn left just before entering the village and continue uphill past the church. At the road junction at the top of the hill turn left again heading towards Weymouth. Eventually you will reach a roundabout at which you turn left. Drive through the hamlet of Poxwell and keep

73

going until you reach the signs for Osmington. Turn left and follow the narrow road to its end in the tiny hamlet, known as Osmington Mills, where you will find a car park opposite a fine old inn. Not for nothing in bygone days was it known as it is today...*The Smugglers* (or "The Smuggs," to locals).

Forget beachcombing for a few moments and sample the delights of the "Smuggs." I'll wager you'll not leave this hostelry easily once having caught sight of the food on offer and sampled the ale!

Having torn yourself away from all that the "Smuggs" has to offer, return to the car park and look across to your left. Here you will see the remains of a ship that was wrecked on this rocky shore many years ago. Turning to your right, you will be confronted by a view of several miles of interesting beach. The path (see Page 78) from the car park where you are now standing was once the primary route of local smugglers bringing ashore their illicit cargoes to the Smugglers Inn, the centre of a thriving trade in these parts.

In summer this area is swarming with day-trippers and tourists, not to mention bathers, so modern finds are well in evidence. At low water an expanse of rocky out-crops looks like forbidding territory, but searching it thoroughly with a small-diameter searchcoil, say 4-inches, can repay handsomely. One distinct advantage of less hospitable terrain is that the density of ring-pulls is much reduced...and the amount of other modern trash. This allows lower discrimination levels and settings, and a "wider net" for desirable finds. Next stop, still moving west, is a famous landmark and hunting ground.

Chesil Beach

The *Chesil* is 22 miles of steeply shelving shingle bank, and for most of its length, arrow straight. The beauty and glory of this area is best appreciated from Portland, a high vantage point where in the right conditions it is possible to overlook the whole length of Chesil Beach...in fact to see almost to Lyme Regis on the western border of Dorset. My words are inadequate, you really must see it for yourself high up from the slopes of Portland to appreciate it's true splendour.

A previous chapter described how coins and artifacts can be sorted and dumped according weight and size by the actions of the tide, waves and longshore drift, but the whole of Chesil Beach is a perfect example of this grading...but on *the grand scale*. The phenomena of the shingle is strange and impressive. At the Portland end the stones are large, some weighing in excess of two pounds, while the stones steadily reduce in size and weight the farther west one travels towards Bridport, where the average size is no greater than a pea. But out to sea, the pattern is reversed! It is said that local fishermen, should they be forced to beach their craft in rough weather or fog, can tell exactly where they are by looking at the size of the pebbles.

The Chesil is at once stunningly impressive and dangerous. Every year it claims the lives of swimmers in its strong currents, and the lives of anglers sucked into the sea. The steep shingle bank is soft underfoot and breaking waves undermine seemingly solid support permitting the unfortunate unwary fisherman to be swept back into the sea. Just four or five feet out, the water will be deep, and those wearing heavy winter gear, or waders, may have little chance of survival.

Beachcombers of yesteryear, searching here with "eyes only" and without all of the

Chesil Beach viewed from Portland is shown at top, with Lulworth Cove, scene of Napoleon's "landing," at bottom.

sophisticated equipment of today always searched the Chesil in pairs and roped themselves together. One would search along the waterline braving the pounding surf, while the other walked along the top of the shingle bank, ready to haul his companion to safety should he lose a foothold.

I would not recommend beachcombing on the Chesil in anything other than calm and settled weather. For anyone walking or hunting along the shoreline during a strong on-shore "blow" (southwesterlies) the risk of drowning is indeed a very real threat. Please don't do it. Even during the heady months of high summer, keep off the Chesil during southwesterly gales.

A Chesil Story

The beach has been the scene of countless wrecks, and many coins and pieces-of-eight have been found here. A favourite and salutary story concerning the Chesil involves a local fisherman who found a piece-of-eight,

Tourists and smugglers alike have left treasures that await THers along this pathway from car park to beach at Osmington.

but did not realise exactly what it was. However, he did know that silver coins can be made into attractive signet rings, so he took the coin to a nearby silversmith who made a good job of it.

Only after the ring had been completed did the owner finally discover that the coin was indeed, very valuable. Now, transformed into a ring, it was worth only a mere fraction of it's true value "as found." Always, and I really do mean, *always,* take expert advice about the identity and value of any coin-like object you find in this locale, and always too, seek that advice from a coin dealer, never a museum.

A similar story relates to a local man who one day found a large black "pebble" weighing more than five pounds on the beach near to Abbotsbury. For the next 10 years this object gave the man truly sterling service as a doorstop for the back door of his cottage. One Sunday lunchtime, his wife asked him to sharpen the carving knife. Unable to locate his usual sharpening stone, the husband decided to see whether the doorstop had some other useful property in addition to sheer weight.

It did. At the first stroke of the blade on the "pebble," it became obvious that it was not made of stone. Later, it was determined that the object was, indeed, made of silver...that it was a tarnished and rounded ingot, worth many thousands of pounds.

Again, when hunting hereabouts, always inspect any large well-rounded black stones, for many ingots still await discovery.

In 1748 the *Hope of Amsterdam*, carrying (then) £50,000 in gold, was wrecked close to Abbotsbury, and it is not known whether all her cargo was salvaged. Certainly our treasure hunting forebears searched the beach, hunting eyes-only for the gold, and in the manner already described. It is doubtful whether they recovered it all.

The Chesil is a complex beach with many moods that are sometimes difficult to comprehend. One man who knows the beach and it's idiosyncrasies better than most, is Bill Irvine, proprietor of Search Southward at 12 Landsdowne Road, Bothenhampton, near Bridgport. Anyone intending to search the "Chesil" for a first time would do well to chat with him before setting out. If he can spare you half an hour, and he's the sort of man who will if he can as he's always willing to talk "treasure," a half hour in Bill's company could be the best and most interesting half hour of your beachcombing life!

Weymouth

Dorset's premier coastal resort, is hardly "off the beaten track" but in winter its beaches can offer empty search areas and some fine artifacts, ranging from gold guinea pieces, sovereigns and early Victorian trinkets to the more mundane objects of the 20th century. The secret, of course, is knowing where to look. To shorten the odds in your favour, I recommend that you locate the clock-tower that dominates the promenade and, at low tide, with this fine marker at your back, walk out onto the exposed sand. When you reach a point where your feet leave no imprint, begin searching. If the water is on the ebb, follow the receding tide right out to DLW, working your detector in a pattern parallel to the promenade. Here, in this area, I can almost guarantee that you will find gold in one form or another!

The Dorset coastline is without doubt a Mecca for beachcombers. If treasure hunters when they shuffle from this mortal coil, go to heaven...as I'm sure they do...

Then heaven, I suspect, won't be too far from Dorset!

Chapter Six

Selsey

The village of Selsey is situated on the promontory known as Selsey Hill and is a thriving summer resort favoured particularly by those holidaymakers who prefer to self-cater. This tourist business is superimposed on the thriving local "industry" of inshore fishing. Many holiday-makers will be beach and boat anglers, and a smaller band of visitors during a much extended "season." Out of season, better still, can be found treasure hunters "in the know." Several valuable coins, Celtic staters, have been recovered from this area by beachcombers using metal detectors.

Here there is fast erosion of the foreshore, aided by strong tides, and landslips onto the beaches are quite common. The mass of material tumbled onto the beach brings new ground in reach of detectors, often containing coins that would not be expected in the natural course of searching a beach, as was the case with the aforementioned Celtic staters.

The popularity of the area with today's holidaymakers also means that finds of modern coins and jewellery can be expected. In fact, it is difficult to guess just what may turn up under your searchcoil.

Searching the exposed foreshore at low water is by far the best plan of action if you seek old gold and rings. Here in particular, the deep-seeking qualities of a pulse induction metal detectors really come into their own. This particular foreshore is almost tailor-made for these types, none more so than the Garrett Sea Hunter, a top flight pulse, that I managed to borrow for the purpose from Regton's Nigel Ingram. (And why not? We writers have to have some 'perks', eh?) To the west, brings to...

Hayling Island

Hayling, like Selsey, is immensely popular with holiday-makers, and in consequence the beaches are loaded with all sorts of their losses. In winter car-parking is no problem at all, but you will not find it easy to buy a hot drink.

One of the best places to hunt is the area close to the lifeboat station where the beach

The Solent

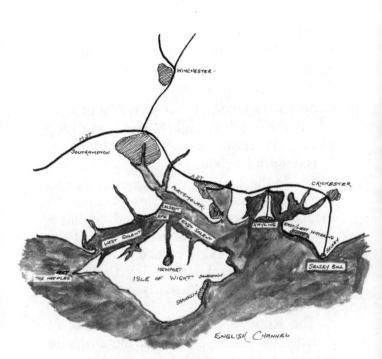

Tidal Range: 13 ft. Springs, 5-10 ft. Neaps

is a mixture of fine sand and light shingle. Curiously, I have recovered several Victorian florins from this locale, especially at DLW and at the farthest possible point that the water will allow...out on the exposed foreshore. The groynes too (wooden structures set up to prevent beach erosion) are most definitely worth inspection. All manner of items are trapped by them--as is a lot of junk, of course--and as rightly they say "Oop North," *Where there's muck, there's brass.*

Portsmouth Harbour

Inside the harbour is Portchester Castle, itself a Scheduled Ancient Monument which means it is expressly out of bounds to detector users. But the foreshore in front of the castle is not so restricted and is well worth searching. Several interesting finds have come from here, particularly artifacts from the Napoleonic era.

The Romans built a fort on the site of Portchester Castle. Although the structure you see today is much later, the Emperor Carausius built fortifications here in about 375 A.D. Coins found by beachcombers suggest that the fort was occupied by the military for only some thirty years...bronze coins of Allectus and early coins of Theodosius, then a gap to coins of much later emperors. 18th-

Century musket balls abound here as do military buttons from the period.

Next we travel north along the shorelines of Southampton Water.

Lee-on-Solent

A favourite coin hunting location of mine, can be found down by the beach huts at the northern end. Here I have found many, many pre-decimal coins...Victorian Half-Crowns, Florins and any amount of pennies, some dating to 1797. For me at least this area has provided a beachcombing bonanza.

The older coins and artifacts are to be found on that part of the foreshore uncovered at DLW. If your particular metal detector has a constant, yet faintly-audible threshold, then you should dig ALL signals that cause this tone to increase, even slightly. Here then, with little or no advance of the discrimination control, save for just a touch to overcome small ferrous objects, you will be working on the very extremes of depth penetration...down there amongst the *oldies!*

Here too is ample free car parking in winter, but as usual in the off-season, little in the way of refreshment facilities. Providing for your own needs is very much the order of the day. And, it's well worth it, especially so on those bitter cold cloudless winter days when this beach is a pure delight...when a fresh-brewed mug of tea so enhances the enthusiasm.

Farther north is perhaps the most under-rated tidal estuary of them all, with the potential to outstrip even, the River Thames foreshore as Britain's number one spot for finding things ancient.

The River Itchen

This heavily silted and muddy backwater must contain many, many ancient artifacts, and unfortunately, most of them may never surrender to our efforts because they lie deep in soft, muddy sludge. Such conditions make it almost impossible, and dangerous, for the beachcomber to operate. But all is not lost! There are some areas of hard-packed shingle that can be worked, which do give up some nice collectables. Netley foreshore is one such location.

Almost anywhere within the foreshore of Southampton's dockland can be expected to produce a varied selection of interesting artifacts. It is an exciting area with huge tracts, as yet, little explored.

Hythe

In our travels down the western side of Southampton Water the tidal foreshore of Hythe should not be passed by. At DLW, under or close to the pier, you will come across many 17th Century and 18th Century clay-pipe bowls. Some of the more ornately designed ones are indeed highly collectible. You are likely to find coinage of dates spread across many centuries, all lying within inches of the surface. It is a fascinating place for the collector.

Pre-decimal coinage abounds, with the odd "hammered"'silver coin turning up here and there, and with Saxon coinage prominent among the older finds. Hythe also is the manufacturing base of Ken Frampton, maker of the famous "Wychwood" display cases, custom built for the display of detector-found artifacts. Highly recommended, they come, too.

Farther down the "Water" we come to the former home of the Supermarine Company, builders of the now legendary fighter plane, the Spitfire. Though the aircraft were built in nearby Woolston, the Supermarine prototypes were flown from our next port of call.

Calshot Spit

It was here too that the Schneider Trophy-winning seaplanes, were tested, antecedents of R.J. Mitchell's design for the Spitfire. Today an Adventure Centre run by the local council operates on the original base of these planes. There is a certain irony in the fact that a council here employing archaeologists have done their utmost to prevent the use of metal detectors along Hampshire's foreshores, even challenging Home Office guidelines on the matter. They have often acted in a manner recalling the propagandist posturing of a foe vanquished by the legendary "Spit," as they use its former base for encouraging a wider public awareness and involvement in marine activities with the exception of the sea's oldest traditional craft...beachcombing.

At low tide, a vast expanse of accessible shingle is exposed. I know of one Phoenician coin that has come from these banks, lending support to amateur theories about trade between the Phoenicians and the Romans and the possible importance of Calshot as a landing place during the Roman and probably Celtic era.

Without hard evidence to the contrary, or interest in supporting evidence, the proposition is dismissed, it seems, by Hampshire's archaeologists following, apparently, the "party line" of opposition to the use of metal detectors by anyone not a member of the archaeology clique. If, eventually, the amateur case is proved, it will be a familiar example of professional and political ambitions distorting the judgment of publicly funded academics.

Moving west brings us to an old battleground for County archaeologists and users of metal detectors.

Lepe

Lepe is ostensibly a country park by the sea, but Hampshire County Council seems upset by the many "public" activities on this foreshore. Maintaining a dismal record of opposition to our pastime, the Council sought to ban digging in the sand by bait-diggers (anglers) and beachcombers, on the pretext that this would threaten a population of wading birds. The wading birds are very hard to find...perhaps these creatures are more concerned about licensed guns, or being mown down by the thousands of windsurfers who have an equal right to be on this stretch of coast.

At the time of writing, by-laws necessary to enforce a general exclusion of metal detecting have not been sanctioned by the Home Office, and there is no reason to suppose that they ever will be! But the discouragement level is high because bigots, more reasonable members of the Council and their officers act as though metal detecting is outlawed from this pleasant Hampshire "outback." The battle must continue, but it is one most readers might prefer to avoid. Fortunately some old campaigners do not feel the same, and one of my treasure hunting friends, who also happens to be a Council member, is actually looking forward to the day when an official tries to impress him with non-existent regulations!

Isle of Wight

There exists on this island a beachcomber who finds so many items of jewellery that the local police no longer take his finds into the custody of their Lost Property Office. Instead, they are content to receive a description of the recovered articles, and then refer any likely claimants to the finder, in person. The system works.

For this man, at least, it is possible to fully savour the pleasure of returning a treasured possession to its owner. Despite opportunist instincts required of, and recommended for, successful beachcombers it is difficult to understand how anyone can gain pleasure from illicitly selling a wedding band which is likely to be of far greater value to its owner than its scrap gold content. Beachcombing for excitement, profit, historical research or the urge to collect are all justifiable and honourable elements of the pastime. But not if they override all concern for other human beings, their property and its personal value.

Generally, beachcombers and treasure hunters have a good record in this respect, but no hobby, sport, occupation or profession has a monopoly of honesty and integrity. The way in which recoveries of modern valuables are handled has a powerful negative or positive influence on general attitudes to the hobby. Opponents to our chosen recreation would have the public at large believe that all thieves are beachcombers, which, may of course be true. *But, all beachcombers are most definitely not thieves!* There is a subtle difference...one which highlights the rabid disinformation being spread about.

Almost every accessible stretch of Island Coast is likely to be another repository of lost modern coins and jewellery. The towns of Ryde, Shanklin, Ventnor and Yarmouth have beaches of long-standing popularity, and thus, rich deposits.

Searching in the vicinity of the famous landmark of the Needles, you should have the possibility of older treasure in mind, perhaps gold or silver coins, or other relics, from a 17th Century shipwreck. This is one source of coins washed ashore and found quite regularly in past years. To stand the best chance of such recoveries, place yourself due south in the bay immediately next to this famous group of rocks, and work the low tide line as close to the Needles as possible.

Hengistbury Head

Returning to the mainland and following the coast to the Christchurch area we come to Hengistbury Head, once the fortress of the Celtic tribal leader Hengist. Metal detectors can still pick up evidence from the period to which the landmark owes its name in the form of items such as Celtic coins and gold leaf. An archaeological excavation is in progress on the Head itself...obviously territory off-limits to amateurs armed with metal detectors, unless invited on by whoever is directing the dig. It's a possibility. So is being struck by lightning.

Nevertheless, important archaeological finds are always a possibility, which you should report first to the Receiver of Wreck

Top: Castle Inn's landlord feeds and waters treasure hunters and also provides a mine of local information at West Lulworth .

Bottom: Wintertime at Weymouth, with the Clock Tower marker visible at the extreme left of the picture.

and then, I recommend, to the local archaeological unit...and, in that order. The sequence is important to protect your own interests. Because you will be dealing, in part, with Hampshire County Council, it is sensible to ask yourself whether any group persuaded to adopt anti-detecting policies is likely to advertise or reward any useful contribution by their supposed adversaries. And, if you think there is any possibility that the find has high monetary value, put your interests in the hands of a solicitor. Ignore this advice at your peril!

It should be added that the supply of information to the archaeological unit is no more than a courtesy gesture, and an expression of tenuous faith that the information will be well used. The interpretation of whether an item could be of archaeological importance is, initially, up to you, and as you become more involved with this hobby, your interpretation

Top: At Poole Harbour beachcombers with metal detectors can find relics from ancient Viking raiders and modern windsurfers alike.

Bottom: Sandbanks, at the entrance to Poole Harbour, is an excellent coinshooting venue, especially along the concrete wall.

is likely to become better. This is the real-world situation ignored by ridiculous propositions for compulsory reporting of "archaeological objects." Needless to say, such propositions have not been offered with any legally useful definition of "an archaeological object," and never will be.

Bournemouth and Boscombe

These are probably two of the finest coin hunting beaches in all Britain, and summertime is the best for raking modern currency. Just after 5 p.m. on a mid-summer's day, when most trippers have left to join their transport home, you stand the best chance of beating the locals at their own game. It would not be at all unusual for a slick operator to leave the beach after an evening's hunting with upwards of £10 to £15 in cash and a couple of rings or other similar trinkets.

The first target area is the sea wall where many people will have been sitting during the day. Work your way along its base before searching further afield.

Poole Harbour

Make straight for Rockley Sands! Follow the road through the holiday camp and you will come to the beach. Get out into the water and begin searching at least 10 yards out, where you will discover that the water is still only ankle deep. Here you can expect to find all manner of coins from all periods. If you are on holiday in the area, but not actually staying at Rockley, make a point of an evening trip to this spot.

Poole Harbour, its shoreline totaling 126 miles, is the second largest natural harbour in the world (second only to Sydney Harbour). There are scores of bays and inlets along this shoreline and all will repay careful inspection. Viking raiders made frequent forays here, sailing up to the town of Wareham, which suffered several sackings by these fierce Norsemen. Today, however, Viking dominance has given way to the ubiquitous wind-surfing fraternity.

The beach area at the eastern side of the harbour's entrance, known as Sandbanks, rivals Bournemouth in the coin hunting stakes in summer. I remember one summer morning, arriving on the beach at 4 a.m. with temperature already up in the 60's and recovering within two hours in excess of £10 and a six-pack of Guinness, the latter having been deliberately buried in the sand to keep cool and subsequently "lost" by one thirsty sun-seeker. On that hot morning, I remember well, toasting my success and his loss!

South Wales
Tidal Range: 7 to 25 ft.

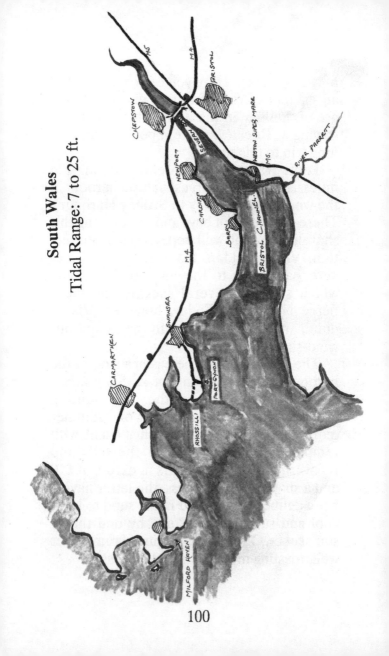

CHEPSTOW

M4

M5

BRISTOL

M4

NEWPORT

SEVERN

WESTON SUPER MARE

M5

RIVER PARRETT

CARDIFF

BARRY

BRISTOL CHANNEL

CARMARTHEN

SWANSEA

M4

RHOSSILI

PORT EYNON

MILFORD HAVEN

100

Chapter Seven

Gower Peninsula

One coast more than any other in Britain is notorious for the number of shipwrecks, not all accidental, that have scattered treasure across its shoreline. The Gower peninsula, South West Wales, is rocky and dangerous, not just for ships, but also for searchers including the "hard men" who take an almost masochistic pleasure in braving the elements and tough terrain, to search the wilder parts of coastline. Here, they reason, the losses will be less accessible to most of their competitors, and if signals are hard to come by, they are worth digging because the levels of modern trash will be much reduced.

Putting theory into practice is not recommended to beachcombing novices, the foolhardy or those not physically strong. They are likely to come to grief. Determination is another required characteristic...you must be prepared to come away with nothing, yet be prepared to go back again and again. For "out there" lies a vast quantity of treasure, particularly Spanish treasure. Perhaps most tantalising of all is one huge stretch of sand which on a fine summer's day may seem awesome only in size. Here, somewhere, there must be more silver Spanish dollars from the 300-year-old wreck at Rhossili. Though most recent organised "mass assaults" by detector users have found some interesting items, Spanish dollars were not amongst them. But, try this beach in a winter gale, and it is a different proposition altogether...frightening territory, indeed, though chances of success may be much improved after layers of sand have been ripped away.

To reach the treasure house of the Gower peninsula from the north or east, you must get yourself to Swansea and follow the signs to the Mumbles. On the coast to the left of your line of travel there are vast mud flats that become exposed at DLW, and almost any part of this area will produce coins and jewellery...ancient if you are lucky and modern more probably since Mumbles remains a popular summer resort. Moving westwards you come to Oxwich Bay, an area you should find rich in coins from all ages, particularly if you care to restrict your searches to the soft dry sand at the top end of the beach.

Nearly all the bays and coastal villages to be mentioned have car parking facilities and most will require a modest fee.

Port Eynon

Continuing west from Oxwich, be alert for the signpost to Port Eynon, which will send you left off the Rhossili road. Port Eynon is a pleasant little village and the new car park on the front gives a good view of the beach, bay and foreshore. The fine dry sand at the top end of the beach (we always assume it is not raining; have a nice day) and adjacent to the fencing by the dunes, is a good spot to begin. Lots of modern coinage is the obvious target here...to pay for all the car parking!

At low water you will see a vast area of rocks and rockpools plus the remains of a ship that ran aground here many years ago. In this locality there is much iron of all shapes and sizes, probably ballast and bolts from the wreck or others that have foundered hereabouts. False signals as your detector responds to this iron have to be endured. But if you are prepared to put up with this not inconsiderable annoyance, then you will find some interesting collectables.

On the borderline where the rocks give

way to sand there is another interesting area. Here, in the past, I have had a number of older coins, some dating well into the Victorian era, and some, much older! Further out on the sand, up to the DLW mark, you should begin to turn up more recently lost items, jewellery and coins, washed out from closer to the high traffic areas of the beach. At this point too, you will almost surely meet a sour-faced individual, also using a detector, who regards this beach and contents as his personal property. Still, it takes all sorts eh?

Leaving Port Eynon, not necessarily for the last reason, follow the road back to the Rhossili junction, turn right, then first left, and follow the roadsigns to Llangennith. Now we are approaching the westerly tip of the Gower, and the sands of silver dollars.

Llangennith

Drive through the village and turn left onto the minor road that leads to a caravan park. Follow the road through the park until you come to a parking area next to the huge sand dunes.

Now is the time to check all of your gear and make sure you have gathered together everything you will need, for there is a longish hike to follow. Take the pathway from the car park and head out towards the sea, across the dunes. When you reach the beach you will be confronted with a breathtaking panorama...a vast, sandy bay some four miles long. If the tide is at DLW, the sea will be almost a quarter of a mile away!

Looking to the distant left you will see a shimmering expanse of wet sand, caused by a fresh water stream which runs onto the beach at this point. This area is called Diles Lake. To your distant right you will see a rocky promontory known as Bury Holmes, and a spit of rocky foreshore which, when covered by the tide, cuts Bury Holmes from the mainland. (This foreshore is known as Spaniards Rocks.) Between Diles Lake and Bury Holmes at, unfortunately, a vaguely specified point beneath the sands, lies the wreck of a Spanish galleon lost here three centuries ago complete with her cargo of silver dollars.

In the early part of the 18th Century the sands shifted to reveal the remains of the galleon, whereupon locals gathered on the beach to scoop up quantities of silver dollars. The bonanza was short lived as the next two tides covered the wreck once more. It is supposed that the wreck was never seen again. Rumours persist that more of the coins still come to light, some from the area of Spaniards Rocks, and some from the sands along the DLW line. Whatever the truth it seems inevitable that more silver dollars will come from hiding somewhere on this vast expanse of sand.

The "Dollar Ship of Rhossili" has inspired many treasure hunts, and every advance in detecting equipment raises new expectations of success. Some determined researchers have trailed proton magnetometers from small boats, hoping to trace the outline of the wreck, but if there has been any success it has been kept very quiet. However, the signals I have read on the "jungle telegraph" within the treasure hunting fraternity strongly suggests that two Swansea-based hunters have done rather well in the suspected areas.

Blue Pool

Rounding the point at Bury Holmes brings you eventually to the small bay, Blue Pool, which takes its name from the seemingly bottomless rockpool within. In truth, the rockpool is some 25 feet deep and, as the name suggests, the water appears blue. It is alleged that one or two gold coins have been found on the floor of the pool, but it is not clear how the finders got there. The bay's main claim to fame is the fair number of gold coins that have become lodged in the cracks and crevices of the surrounding cliffs. It seems more than probable that a wreck of some kind lies just offshore, and that the coins have been thrown up into the cliffs during storms and rough weather.

A necessary word of caution: This bay is the very model for earlier warnings about the dangers of being cut off from safety by the tide. It presents a very real danger, and you need the appropriate maps and tide tables for this area and time of year. Figures given elsewhere are no more than examples of how calculations should be made from the local, timely data.

Usually, winter-times on the Gower Coast can be bitingly cold, especially when the wind is up and raging. Since there is not much to be found in the way of cafes at this time of year, you need to carry plenty of food and...better still, if you have a means of producing it...hot food. In Llangenthith, the local hostelry opposite the church does a nice line in "pub grub" served at the bar and also provides good accommodation at reasonable prices. It would make a good base from which to explore this exciting part of the coast.

So the Gower Coast can be a very special and exciting weekend target for treasure hunters, especially the more active and level-headed. Before you make this pilgrimage I recommend that you obtain a copy of George Edmund's authoritative book, *The Gower Coast,* a treasure store of information with more than enough leads to follow than in this more general book of mine.

Pembroke and Milford

Excellent! The Dartmouth of South Wales. Milford is all that you expect from a quality seaside town, with lots of ample car-parking (in winter at least) of the pay-and-display type, a host of cafes to get yourself a cuppa or three, and beaches which offer endless hours of enjoyment for the searcher, winter or summer.

The estuary and its backwaters cry out for investigation. Many old ferries have long since vanished, but the foreshores where they onloaded and offloaded (where money changed hands) are well worth the effort of finding and searching. The backwater villages of Landshipping and Newton Mountain must in their past have welcomed man-powered ferries carrying livestock and people. This pleasant backwater is certainly a future target of mine, and I don't much care whether I find the hammered coinage first (indicating a ferry site) or the ferry site as an hors d'oeuvre for the coinage!

That is the extent of our southwestern

travels. Now we shall head for the Severn Estuary and the English Borders. But one stop must be made on the way.

Barry Island

We cannot pass this by because Barry Island is a first-class treasure hunting location, an area that has always come up trumps for me, best of all in winter. It is not the most bustling of places off-season, but provides good parking and a scattering of comfortable eating places and more modest cafes.

Anywhere on Barry's beaches, mostly of fine sand, will turn up a great variety of items. Working with your detector below the high water mark can uncover some very smart pieces of jewellery indeed. This is a popular and accessible beach for treasure hunting, so it can hardly be described as "off the beaten track." You're likely to have company if searching at the week-end!

There is a story of one lucky searcher who came across a glory-hole somewhere near here, pulling out modern coins to a total value of more than £100 from one small patch of sand. Such freak collections of finds are well attested to, exceptional by definition, but if you've found a couple of coins in one spot, keep at it right there: it could just be your turn!

The Severn

The River Severn has witnessed trading vessels traveling its length since before recorded history, and today large cargo vessels still cross its waters. The territory is huge and no doubt deserves its own tome written by a local specialist. I simply call your attention to one spot that has drawn mine.

To reach it from the east you must leave the M4 Motorway at the Chepstow turn-off, then follow the roadsigns for the B4228, doubling back towards the Severn Bridge. This time you approach it at "ground level," and you'll be directly underneath it with the Army Apprentices College behind you. You need to reach this point at least two hours before DLW, when the water to your left will retreat to expose a huge reef.

This reef is covered with slimy weed, treacherous stuff, and enough to put off the most determined. There is definitely risk of damaging yourself and your detector if you lose a foothold. But, the reef is attractive to beachcombers because it has caused other damage...putting an end to many rowboat ferries in bygone times. The reef takes some searching out, but all manner of coins have been lost here as recent finds indicate. Roman coins show up now and again and it seems likely that the same crossing point was used in that era. I don't yet know what's on the "English" side of the Severn, opposite, but for sure, a lucrative site exists somewhere there.

Once again, do not let the possibilities of good finds and bad falls cause you to forget that what goes out comes in again...ocean water, gallons of the stuff. It's all to easy to be cut off from any escape route when working the higher ground and immersed mentally, in searching. You may suddenly find yourself in danger of a much more literal and dangerous submersion! If you don't understand tide tables, don't detect here. If you do, you can easily obtain local data in Chepstow.

Across the water, heading south on the M5 Motorway brings you to Weston-Super-Mare, with its vast sands and mud banks. However, good finds can be made near the pier or under it, or close in to the sea wall to the right of the pier. Clevedon, a popular resort in Victorian times, is nearer for Bristolians, but the beaches are pebble not sand. The road to the beach goes through the town whose retailers used to do a brisk trade in buckets and spades, but they were bound to be found out eventually! In Weston on the other hand, there is more sand than anyone can cope with. Below the old promenade wall is an obvious magnet, but the areas to head for are the mudflats further out, freshly stripped of sand by tide and storm. Well south of the beach beyond Barrow and Burnham, is the Parrett estuary, a spot where I have made some good finds.

The Severn Bridge, viewed from the fore-shore of the 14th-Century Old Ferry Inn, where many early coins have been found.

Chapter Eight

The islands of Majorca, Menorca, Ibiza and Formentura make up the world-famous Balearic Islands in the northwest Mediterranean Sea. Governed by Spain, they are aptly known as Europe's number one holiday destination. Millions of tourists visit the islands each year, with some six million Britons alone swelling the ranks of sun-seekers. The Balearics are indeed Europe's playground

Among these millions of visitors must certainly be many beachcombing and other detector enthusiasts who would like, but cannot get access to, information relating to their

Treasures await the finding among gnarled old olive trees that dominate the Mediterranean landscape of the Balearic Islands particular sport hereabouts. Chapter Eight seeks to remedy this situation and to project a starting point for anyone taking a metal detector to this locale.

The quantity and quality of the finds to be made hereabouts are truly staggering. The golden sands of these beautiful islands have proved to hold a king's ransom in coins and jewellery...just waiting to be discovered by someone armed with a metal detector and a little knowledge. In this Chapter we shall be exploring three islands: Majorca, Menorca and Formentura.

Surprisingly, summertime is not the "prime time" for a beachcombing holiday. It is then that beaches are always packed to capacity with acres of lobster-pink flesh toasting away in the sun. There's hardly room to swing the proverbial "cat," let alone a metal detector! Of course, beaches packed to capacity hold no terrors to the astute beachcomber, for he (or she) hunts when the sun worshipers have long departed...early evening or early morning when the temperatures are much more bearable and comfortable. Still, it is easier to hunt when crowds are not so dense and when one's every move (and treasure discovery) is not under such close observation!

In addition, the blistering heat of high summer, makes for a most uncomfortable time when hunting, particularly when wearing headphones. Beads of sweat will run into your ears and headphones, attracting the flies and gnats, akin to wasps around a jam pot! By far the most *comfortable* time of year is from October through the following April when, the air is crisp and warm and the beaches almost deserted. Even the flies will be "holidaying" elsewhere.

Majorca

Largest of the Balearics, Majorca is, roughly, 50 miles long and some 40 miles across, with a range of high mountains, the Sierras de Tramuntaña to the north. This mountain range is what makes Majorca so pleasant and dry in winter, draining the rain clouds of their load before sweeping inland. The name Majorca is derived from the Roman "major" meaning big, and "orca", meaning island. Thus, Majorca means literally, *big island.* Similarly, Menorca comes from the Roman "min"and means *little island.*

Ideally, a car is by far the best and most reliable way of getting about on Majorca and these can be hired quite readily and reasonably cheaply if you care to shop around. The best bet though, is to book a car through the same company with which your holiday was booked, via the travel courier. This should ensure that you get a car in a roadworthy condition. The term "roadworthy" in Majorca means that the vehicle is capable of moving forward and backward, has four wheels (sometimes) and an engine! Majorcan hire-cars have to be seen to be believed! But after you have driven on some of the backroads and experienced the thrill driving along potholed carriageways whilst simultaneously negotiating partially blocked

Majorca

mountain passes due to rockfalls and landslips, it will soon become patently clear why some of the hire-cars are in the condition they are! Look upon it as part of Majorca's "laid-back" atmosphere...an experience.

Almost any beach on the island will produce vast quantities of coins. Fact! However, if you are looking for older-type coins, then you must get away from the holiday beaches, and head up into the mountains (and down again) to a place called...

La Calobra

A tortuous 14-kilometre road complete with hairpin bends (and kamikaze sheep) turns off the main mountain road and winds its way down to this idyllic hamlet by the sea. Follow the road into the "village" past the excellent cafe on the right next to the orange grove, and you will arrive at a car park. From the car park follow the footpath until you are confronted by a "Y" junction. Take the right-hand path, and using the torch you brought with you, negotiate the tunnel in the cliff-face.

Emerging from the tunnel on the far side, you will be confronted with what was once a natural harbour...although, since Roman times it has become heavily silted. A river meanders down into the sea from the mountains in the gorge that widens out here to form this natural harbour. The gorge revels in the nickname of Majorca's Grand Canyon, and like the real one, is an awe-inspiring sight. You will probably have the sensation of hundreds of hungry eyes boring into you as you reemerge from the tunnel, and of course, there will be…packs of cats perched on rocks watching your every move, waiting, for you to wander off from your lunch-box.

Under no circumstances feed these animals, or get too close to them. They are not pets, and some could be rabid. Once the cats realise they are not going to get any tidbits from you, they will, eventually, wander away. If you have children with you take special care. These creatures may look to all intents and purposes like the good old British domestic "moggy." Yet, they are wild, in every sense…even though they and their kittens can be a magnet to children.

From here make your way to the shingle bar at the mouth of the cove. This will require you to wade, albeit only ankle-deep, through the meandering river to reach it. During my last visit here, I spent an hour and a half detecting this shingle bar, after which time I must have had well over 150 coins of all descriptions, including one or two coins from the Middle Ages. This was in addition to a number of items, fashioned in *gold*!

Quite obviously, everything washed down in the river is captured by the shingle bar and is just waiting to be discovered. La Calobra is a glorious place and one that I have visited many times. The shingle bar shelves steeply into the warm gin-clear water, and what treasure must lay at the point where the steep shelving shingle levels off into the sand is not hard to imagine.

Alcudia

If you prefer to have your beachcombing expeditions result predominantly in an end product of spendable cash, then the wide sandy beaches of Alcudia in the north of the island, will more than delight you. Unlike Britain, the Mediterranean Sea has very little tidal movement, consequently very few coins ever get washed into the sea. However, after an on-shore storm many sandy beaches become "stepped" by action of the crashing waves. If you are lucky enough to come across this condition on a beach, particularly at Alcudia, and have the good sense to hunt along the lines of the "steps," parallel to the beach, you will find many, many, coins and other items that would normally have been out of your detector's depth capabilities.

It is possible at Alcudia to wade into the sea for quite some distance before water reaches your knees. Anyone searching with a fully-waterproof or underwater-type machine and armed with a sand-scoop should find some very valuable trinkets indeed. *Gold Belt* might be a more accurate description!

Careful observation shows that most gold and jewellery will be found (at Alcudia at least) round about 150 yards from the beach, at a point where the water comes up between knee and waist level. When bathers are in this depth of water, and most are still standing, incoming waves break over their chests. It is these strong waves that strip rings from fingers and lockets from necks. This principle applies to most other beaches anywhere in the world. Once having observed the distance and depth that this phenomena occurs, begin your search pattern parallel to the main beach.

General Thoughts

As I mentioned in the opening of this chapter, almost any beach on the island will produce coins, but the two that I've briefly described are well worth the effort of a visit. During the course of your visit to Majorca, you may well discover other coves, bays and sandy stretches more to your liking, but the two already described should point you in the right direction for starters.

As in Britain, the concept that all land belongs to someone applies with equal veracity on Majorca. Thus, if you get the urge to try your hand at some inland venue that takes your fancy, a polite enquiry at most farmhouses will secure permission. It has been my experience that presenting the farmer with a bottle of excellent Spanish brandy costing only the equivalent of a couple of pounds, more than pays dividends. This small 'thank you' gift is always greatly received, and moreover, ensures a further day's outing. Word soon gets around amongst neighbouring farmers, some of whom will likely regard your behaviour as eccentric to say the least! In their view, anyone who gives away brandy in return for old coins that can't be spent, MUST be off his trolley!

More seriously and sadly in this modern age in which we live, we are blighted with the horrendous phenomena that is international terrorism, bombings and hijackings of all kinds. Air travelers nowadays are required to undergo intensive baggage checks, out of sheer necessity...inconvenient perhaps, but none the less, vital to air safety.

At air terminal departure points all baggage and hand luggage is screened by x-ray scanners which show the contents of any piece of luggage on a closed-circuit television monitor. I leave to your imagination the events that occur when revealed inside my luggage, and appearing on the television monitor, is a box containing sundry wires connected to a set of batteries!

For the sake of your convenience, and the peace of mind of those charged with the delicate task of inspecting luggage, do tell them that you are carrying a metal detector in your luggage *before* they put it through the screening process. The detector can be easily transported in a custom-made shoulder case, similar in design to the type used for carrying shotguns. (These shoulder bags too, can draw anxious looks from an alert security staff!)

Most airlines will allow you to take the bag with the metal detector on board the aircraft, and the cabin staff will usually, as has been my experience, take the bag from you and stow it safely, somewhere out of harm's way.

These small but important points all make for a smoother holiday. It certainly won't help to get you in the holiday mood as you watch anxious security men carrying out a controlled explosion on your metal detector! Assuming that you have passed through all the security checks with ease, let's take a look at what the other islands have to offer.

Menorca

The second largest island of the Balearics chain, Menorca, is perhaps, apart from Formentura, the most under-commercialised of them all, shunning the high-rise developments that many people reckon scars the natural beauty of most Spanish resorts. The holiday leisure complexes of Menorca, based on the ancient pueblo system, are laid out and built in a fashion that thousands of holidaymakers find attractive enough to keep

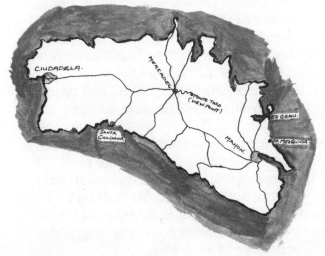

Menorca

pulling them back year after year. Next to Formentura, Menorca is one of my own favourite spots.

A common complaint made by some people holidaying here for the first time is that there is little to do in the evenings. Discos and other haunts so beloved by the lager-swilling, "ere we go, ere we go," brigade for whom vomiting on pavements is part and parcel of a Spanish holiday and generally contributing to Britain's less than salubrious national image abroad, are very much the exception rather than the rule. On Menorca, an evening stroll along the harbour front at Mahon, stopping now and again at any one of the many cafes for a "cafe con leche y cognac" and watching the fishing boats and yachts rocking gently at their moorings, can be considered as a riotous night on the town!

If you like your holidays quiet and peaceful, then Menorca is the place to head for! Self-catering holidays are probably the most suitable for the beachcomber and his family, and very reasonably priced they are too. Due to Menorca's under-commercialisation, very few opportunities exist for holidays off-season. In fact September and October mark the end of the summer holiday season, which starts all over again in early April.

April, May, September and October are the times of the year when Menorca is least likely to be "busy" and, consequently, more attractive to the beachcomber. Of the four months, October is my preference. With temperatures at this time of year still well into the eighties...with the sea already well warmed by the fierce summer sun...with hardly any tourists, the island is sheer delight.

The shallow waters of Es Grau for instance, can be likened to stepping into a tepid bath, which makes for a very pleasant environment in which to while away an hour or two with your metal detector.

So, where to begin? The true answer is almost anywhere! But with that stated, my experience has been that some beaches are better than others. The first place to beat a path to on Menorca is the monastery atop the 1,200-feet-high Monte Torro, from whose balconies you can see over almost the entire island. It's a good place to look at a map and orientate oneself. Don't leave the monastery before having tasted the home-made macaroons, a delicacy which has added to the monastery's world renown. Coffee and macaroons taken on the cafeteria's balcony while enjoying a view hard to equal anywhere, is an experience you'll long remember.

Referring to the map, as you sip your coffee, you will see on the coastline, north of the island's capital Mahon, the bay of...

Cala Mesquida

Probably not one of Menorca's best beaches but certainly one of the most popular, with the locals and tourists alike, Cala Mesquida is a steep shelving sandy beach, that can at times become a little grubby from flotsam washed up during storms. If you can cope with the numerous ring-pulls here, you will have an interesting few hours searching. Moving north a couple of kilometres, will bring you to my all-time favourite beachcombing location.

Es Grau

This beach, in my humble opinion, displays Menorca at its finest...a small fishing community of whitewashed houses beside a most beautiful shallow sandy bay, one in which children can happily splash about all day without coming to any harm.

Here in the dunes at the top of the beach, you can set up the family "base" and enjoy a waterside picnic. This beach is never crowded during September or October and offers plenty of scope for your beachcombing; and more importantly, a safe haven for the children.

It is possible to wade out in the shallow water at least a hundred yards from the shore and even then the water will only be lapping at your knees. With little rubbish save for the odd ring-pull which won't cause too many problems, you can operate your detector with the **Discrim** control turned to the bare minimum. Working along an imaginary line parallel to the shore will produce a number of signals, most of which, if not all, will be either coins or jewellery of some description. Paradise found!

However, to ease retrieval of these items, you will need to use a scoop quite unlike the normal type of beachcomber's trowel...a specially designed sandscoop, a box-like contraption with holes. Once having pin-pointed your signal, drive the scoop into the sand so that the very *signal* itself is lifted into the box section of the scoop. Then, lift the scoop vertically to the surface. Swilling the scoop in the water will rid it of the sand, leaving behind whatever was causing a signal. Obviously, never allow the detector control box to come into contact with the water when hunting in this manner, unless of course you own, as I do, a specially built surf hunting detector.

The sandscoop is the preferred recovery tool when you are hunting in areas of fine dry sand. Once you have pin-pointed the target, scoop up the sand which runs out of the holes like a massive egg-timer, leaving in its basket the metal item of whatever description. Hopefully, not a ring-pull.

Treasure hunting in water, obviously, brings its own unique problems, particularly if you are using a metal detector not especially designated as *All Terrain*. (Submersible, in other words). So, if inadvertently you do by some misfortune immerse your detector in sea water, all is not lost, but, you must act quickly! Remove the batteries and flush the control box in or under fresh water. Particularly, rinse the inside of the control box and thoroughly flush the electronics. Don't worry about damage! It's already had a good dousing of corrosive sea water! Then, once rinsed, shake dry, then dry it out completely using a hair-dryer. When all the moisture has gone, reassemble. Then when you get back to

Top: Ancient remains of Roman salt workings on Formentura hint at the vast storehouse of relic prizes that await THers.

Bottom: This beautiful and expensive diamond solitaire ring was scooped up from a Minorcan beach after a detector found it.

the UK, get it along to the manufacturer, explaining the circumstances. Let them give it a thorough checking over and replace any parts that might be "on the way out."

Whatever you do, never let the seawater dry out. What will happen is that the water will evaporate, leaving behind a residue of corrosive salt which will almost certainly put your metal detector beyond redemption. Indeed, if the worst comes to the worst, and you find that you are unable to get the machine back to your hotel or accommodation immediately, then keep the detector immersed, all day if need be, in sea water. Then, follow the procedure already described.

Once dried, the detector will work, save for the external loudspeaker. Its paper diaphragm will more than likely have dissolved. But not to worry, it's an "extra" hardly ever used anyway; so, no real harm will be done. Of course, ALWAYS switch the detector **OFF** as soon a possible after a dunking, and keep it switched **OFF** until thoroughly dried out.

At this 15th-Century fortification, typical of the Mediterranean, THers can find old buttons, buckles and coins, as well as modern jewelry, such as the bracelet shown below.

If you are some distance from your holiday base, keep the detector immersed in seawater (batteries removed) for as long a possible prior to your return to your hotel or self-catering apartment. Wrap the detector in a wet towel putting the wet towel and detector into a plastic bag. As long as you keep the detector wet, no real harm will come to it.

A fully waterproof metal detector such as the Beach Hunter AT4 of Garrett Electronics really can't be bettered in beach hunting situations. It has the added advantage that the control box can be belt-mounted and also breaks down small enough to be easily stowed or carried in a small suitcase. It is a metal detector I have no reservations at all in recommending. My views on the AT4, along with other comments about the Garrett line have been already well ventilated. They are to metal detecting what Orvis carbon-fibre rods are to fly fishing…expensive, superbly crafted and a joy to use.

Back to Es Grau! If you will take care to follow the footpath along the beach away from the village, you will reach several coves and small inlets. In all probability, you will have these all to yourself all day long. Indeed, you may well find that Es Grau is so endearing that the rest of your holiday will be spent exploring in and around the bay. No matter how long you stay here, you will have made a good choice. So, save a little for me too!

The southwest coastline has one or two resorts that should not be overlooked either, and the major resort on this stretch is...

Cala Galdana

A gently curving bay of golden sand, Cala Galdana is reckoned by some to be the premier beach on the whole of Menorca. Perhaps so. In the height of the season its fine sandy beach is packed to capacity with bodies gently toasting in the sun, while countless others bask in the shallow waters of the bay cooling off in crystal water.

Quite obviously, even to think about beachcombing during these times is completely out of the question! But, if your personal circumstances dictate that you must take your holidays during the high season, all is not necessarily lost. Searching in the early morning and mid-evening hours when temperatures are that much more conducive to comfortable beachcombing will prove justly rewarding. On this beach you simply cannot fail to find coins. Find one and you'll find 50!

A particular part of Galdana's bay that I can recommend to you based upon my own success is close to the rocks along the northern end of the bay, almost under the bar/cafe nestling up in the cliff-face. In fact, it might be to your advantage to have a beer or three on the cafe's patio. From this vantage-point, you can take in all of the bay, whilst making mental notes of the positions of the natural coin and ring "traps"…in other words, observing where the most concentrated groups of sunbathers are basking…observing where in the water, how far out, how deep, are they paddling, wallowing or just idling. All these mental notes should be made before attempting to hunt.

Transport

Menorca has only one real highway, which traverses the length of the island from Mahon to Cuidadela in the north. From this main arterial road, many smaller roads turn off for the villages on the north and south coasts. Turning off from these roads are minor roads that are little more than glorified cart tracks: rocky and very dusty!

These cart tracks are the heart of the island. Follow them and you will come to the *real* Menorca. The Menorca 99% of visitors never see. This is old country, so take the camera, and don't forget the detector either. If you are given the chance to search in a olive grove, grab it with both hands! Most olive trees live in excess of 300 years, and the groves too, will have changed little in that time. There's many a good coin come from under an olive tree, I can tell you!

In order to see as much of the island as time will allow, you must have your own transport, either in the form of a car--or better still, if there are just two of you, a scooter. As in Majorca, these can be easily hired locally or through your travel-company courier on arrival. Local buses are good and cheap, but have the distinct disadvantage of not being able to get close to the locations that you will have in mind.

When your time comes to leave the island, irrespective of whether it's been a beach-combing success or not, you will want to return. To realise the potential of the beaches, I have always found enough hard cash to more than pay for my day to day expenses. I well remember one stay in Menorca when for the first seven days I never touched my bank roll! Vino, the evil weed and a couple of nights out sampling the local gastronomic delights...all came courtesy of the local beaches. So blase was I, that I used to pop down to the nearby beach at 5 a.m., make a "withdrawal" from my "account," then spend the rest of the day touring the island studying "form" (the kind important to beach-combers, rather than the bronzed, long-legged, nubile Teutonic nymphets, who I hardly noticed). Phew!

Formentura

The best has been saved until last! Formentura is the closest many of us will ever come to a desert island, yet this jewel is only an hour's bumpy ferryboat crossing from the gaudy and brash holiday island of Ibiza. In stark contrast to Ibiza's bustling bars, 24-hour discos, neon signs and general hurly burly one would expect from one of Europe's more colourful holiday destinations, Formentura's nightlife extends to the quiet bars and pave-ment cafes of the capital San Francisco, where visitor and islander sip their drinks cheek by jowl. If you can't hack going "native," then Formentura's not for you.

But I, as one whose formative years were spent in the Med, find that going "native" holds no terrors. Rather, it's always a trip down memory lane. Formentura offers the greater scope for beachcombing and is probably one of the best spots to be found anywhere in the Med. Wild and beautiful in all aspects, it most certainly isn't for those who like to boogie the night away. It was only in 1987, for instance, that the island got its first tarmac road! The Island Council has decided wisely to maintain Formentura's traditions and way of life, rather than opt for the "blight" that in my opinion dogs the likes of Benidorm.

The new tarmac road, traverses the island from end to end, some seven miles, while Formentura is about one and one-half miles across at its widest. Little more than the most basic of tracks reach into the interior, tracks that have not changed in 600 years...tracks over which the Barbary Corsairs tramped, when Formentura was their stronghold!

Accommodation on the island is some-

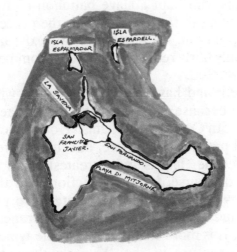

Formentura

what sparse, although very good quality self-catering apartments can be found. Hotels are almost non existent since the island's authorities, anxious to preserve this last bastion of the undisturbed way of island life, have forbidden any building to have more than three stories. The island has no natural water supply, and that which does exist is contaminated with the high saline content of Formentura's soil. This presents no problem, of course, since local shops sell spring-fresh mineral water imported from the Spanish mainland.

Formentura was first colonised by the Romans who kept a slave battalion or two producing salt from seawater by the process of evaporation. These salt pans still exist and until only fairly recently were being commercially worked.

The island has never been popular with settlers because of its water situation. Indeed, in the 15th Century the Spanish Government forced people to live here, but that too fell into decline. The island's greatest claim to fame, of course, is its connection with the Barbary Corsairs, Moorish pirates who pillaged and looted along all the Mediterranean coasts. It is more than likely that the typical pirate treasure of the "X-marks-the-spot" type exists somewhere hereabouts.

By way of passing interest, it was the lighthouse on the eastern tip of the island atop the sheer 350-foot cliffs, that inspired Jules Verne to write his novel of piracy, *The Light at the End of The World.*

During the peak of the tourist season only 20,000 people will be found at any time on the island. Yet, this little island's beaches continue to produce the highest yields of coins and jewellery that I have ever experienced. For example, at a location to be described shortly I recovered 143 coins of all denominations and currencies from a patch of ground just 25 feet by 15 feet, in only about 25 minutes.

Ideally, you will need to use a discriminating metal detector, and a Garrett AT4 fits the bill to a tee. If you don't have access to a waterproof detector, one designed for normal inland usage and protected in a way to exclude dust and sand will do the trick. Of course, you must take care not to immerse the control box housing if you're tempted to hunt a little way out in the surf.

You will also need a sandscoop and a small sharp trowel, built along the lines of the American "Alligator" trowel. Here on Formentura you will be hunting in high trash areas of sand dunes and picnic spots, using an orthodox trowel, and the sandscoop for the beach itself and in the water.

In the way of clothing, wear a baseball type cap together with a pair of sunglasses along with sensible footwear to protect your feet from broken glass, and occasional discarded hypodermic needles. The "hypo" is fast becoming one of the most oft-found pieces of seaside trash. With the risk of accidentally piercing a foot or finger, ALWAYS carry a strong antiseptic and apply it IMMEDI-ATELY if you do draw blood in an unforeseen encounter. In any case, get speedy and qualified help, particularly with the threat of the AIDS virus everpresent in discarded needles.

Now we'll take a closer look at a couple of the island's beachcombing hotspots.

To the north of the island, the Ibiza side, where the beaches are magnificent and sand is golden, most items dropped onto the surface are quickly swallowed by the fine sand. The "top" end of these beaches slowly merges into an area of grassy sand dunes, before these too, give way to the huge acreage of cypress groves, much in evidence on this side of the island.

It is in these groves that the best coins are

to be found, literally thousands of them. From an area under a large and gnarled old cypress tree, I recovered 143 coins of varying denominations of French, Spanish, English, German and Dutch origins, with some dating back to early this century...all of this in the space of just under 25 minutes! Of course the bulk of this haul was predominantly recent and Spanish. These coins, nevertheless, once washed and scrubbed, were immediately spendable.

The abundance of coinage in this area was not straight away obvious, but following some detective work grilling the locals, all was soon revealed. It is a long-standing custom for the locals to gather with their families every Sunday for a family picnic and barbecue, with grandparents, aunts and uncles, wives and husbands and the children. While the children play close by, the adults engage in animated discussion, drinking wine or dozing off in the shade of the groves fanned by the warm sea breezes. Only mad dogs, as they say, and Englishmen go out in the midday sun! Thus, the cypress groves are a high-traffic area in comparison to the beaches hereabouts.

Glancing at the map of Formentura, the site of the old windmill (now a splendid bar) near the "point" of the island, makes an excellent reference point to begin a search of the groves close by. When you visit this area you cannot fail to notice the offshore reef which runs parallel to the beach for some distance, and some 25 yards out in only 4 feet of water. This reef, beach side, is a vault of jewellery. The environment is tailor-made for the Garrett AT4, or indeed any fully waterproof detector. Beach Hunter users should be advised to equip themselves with a set of waterproof headphones. At some stage during their recovery of finds, it will be necessary to put one's head under water, especially if not in possession of a long-handled scoop. In any case, waterproof headphones should always be worn when wading just in case you miss a foothold and inadvertently take a ducking. The detector will continue to function, that's what it's designed for, but soggy "land" headphones with paper diaphragms tend not to perform at their best! (A fact I can vouch for!)

The southern coastline is predominantly rocky and arid and, not surprisingly, very little in the way of vegetation survives here. There are some small sandy coves and a couple of sandy beaches with easy access, but my experience of searching here has determined that these do not have the same rich deposits as those to the north. Certainly, you will find coins and jewellery, but not I think in the abundance of the northern coasts.

I am sure though that once you have spent a fortnight or so on this delightful island you will want to return again and again. The only other treasure hunter you are likely to meet here will be me. I look forward to seeing you.

And, as Charles Garrett says so aptly...

I'll see you in the water!

Appendix I

During the course of your new hobby you will come across certain terms and perhaps phrases that leave you completely baffled. Like most other hobbies and pursuits, Treasure Hunting has evolved it's own vocabulary and terminology. To help you overcome and understand this 'jargon' the following compendium has been compiled.

In-Air Test — A simple test conducted "in air," usually by passing a coin-sized object under the searchcoil to check an individual detector's depth penetration.

All Metal Mode — A particular type of operation, opposite in performance to the Discriminate mode, in which the detector responds to all metals.

Chatter — Unwanted audio interference caused by junk or iron just under the surface. Can also be caused by heavily mineralised ground conditions.

Target Meter — The visual version of the audio signal. Meters can report whether an object is ferrous or non-ferrous. Some can register the approximate depth of coin-sized objects.

Depth Penetration—The distance at which the detector can transmit its electromagnetic field into the ground.

Drift—Loss of tuning stability after the detector has been *tuned* for maximum performance, at the point known as *threshold.*

Ground Effect—Negative or positive mineralisation of the ground. This condition affects to a greater or lesser degree, according to the amount of mineralisation present in the ground, the performance (stability and depth penetration) of the detector. De-sensitising the detector by adjusting the sensitivity control will alleviate the problem a little.

Hot Rock—Any rock or pebble that is more highly mineralised than the surrounding ground. These rocks will be picked-up by a detector.

Null—The zone below the audible threshold in tuning a metal detector. It also refers to the momentary silent response caused when the searchcoil passes over a rejected target, particularly iron.

Pinpointing—A method of locating the center of the signal under the searchcoil by sweeping the searchcoil one way, then another, in the form of an "X." Sometimes referred to as "X-ing."

Signal — The audio or visual response to a detected target.

THer — Treasure Hunter.

THing — Treasure Hunting.

Threshold — The optimum tuning point of a metal detector. This setting is indicated by a faint humming via the detector's audio output.

Tuning Control — Usually incorporated in the *ON/OFF* switch. This control is adjusted to bring the detector to *Threshold*.

VLF — Very Low Frequency. Refers to detectors that operate between 3kHz and 30kHz.

In addition to the terms already listed which refer to the actual operational aspects of using a metal detector, I have listed a selection of the more common terms used in connection with the hobby itself:

Cowboy — A person who knowingly steals artifacts from protected archaeological sites, usually under the cover of darkness.

Hammered Silver — A medieval silver coin minted by the process of being struck with two dies to imprint the logo's.

149

Pre-Decimal — Refers to any coin, but usually silver coins, dated before 1946 when such coins contained a percentage of silver.

Pre-'47 Silver — As above.

Scheduled Site — An archaeological site or area protected by law and, subsequently out of bounds to metal detector users.

Trench Rat — An archaeologist of dubious reputation known to associate with, and purchase the ill-gotten gains of *Cowboys*. (Both categories are in a minority, but unfortunately, exist.)

Appendix II

The Foreshore (Beach)

The Foreshore is that part of the beach that lies between the *high* and *low* water marks, or that area of the beach that is intermittently covered by the *tides*.

This area belongs to the Crown, except in a few instances where the Crown has sold its ownership rights to private citizens. For the most part, there exist very few private beaches, but it always pays to check for any prohibitive signposts or marker boards in the locality. Thus members of the public, and that includes THers, have no right of access to such private stretches of foreshore.

Equally, foreshores owned by the Crown have similar rights, and you are only allowed access because the Crown chooses to allow access. Strictly speaking then, your access is not a right but a privilege.

Gold and Silver

Any item of gold or silver, found between the high and low water marks, the area that belongs to the Crown, *must* be reported to the Crown's Agent in these matters, **The Receiver of Wreck**, who in effect can be likened to a Coroner, although the Receiver of Wreck's main area of interest is beach-found items. The reporting procedure to a local Receiver is basically the same as dealing with reporting finds to a land-based Coroner. In the first instance, contact the local police, who will then put the wheels in motion.

It is always to your benefit to report objects of gold and silver to the Receiver, but most certainly not to your advantage should you fail to do so, and subsequently be reported!

Trespass

Broadly speaking the definition of trespass is entering upon land owned by another and over which no public right-of-way or access has been granted, either by long-standing statute or by the landowner. It matters not that your trespass was committed unintentionally, the trespass will have been committed, and you are therefore obliged to leave the land forthwith if the owner of the land requests you to do so.

Intentional trespass is most certainly actionable, even though the trespasser *believed* he had a right of way, or right of access.

Broader Concepts

All land everywhere belongs to someone. It is your duty to seek permission before venturing onto any land outside the perimeters of your own property. It is generally accepted that on other than private foreshores, public access is granted, and thus members of the public not liable to prosecution.

Above the High Water Mark

Any finds discovered on a beach are the property of the person who lost them. You have a duty in law to take reasonable steps to return them to the owner, and the generally accepted method is by reporting the find to the local police station. Quite obviously, coins cannot be so returned, thus the law turns a *blind eye*. In the strictest sense of the law even coins must be reported to the authorities. Items of jewellery that have specific identifying marks most certainly must be reported. Failure to do so could result in a prosecution under the Theft Act, 1968, under what is generally known as *stealing by finding*.

This general concept applies with equal force in the Channel Islands as well. Thus, if ever in doubt, always report items of jewellery straight away.

Spain's laws seem to be somewhat different in practice. They seem to have an aversion to report-writing, if my experience is anything to go by. When I once tried to hand in a bracelet to a member of the local police, he assumed I was in the process of offering a bribe! Then having convinced him this was not the case, I was told that it was, "OK, OK, Go!" He shrugged his shoulders, turned and walked away. But the message still is to do that which you would do in Britain.

Appendix III

National Council for Metal Detecting
c/o, Central Council for Physical Recrea-
tion,
Francis House,
Francis Street,
London.

Treasure Hunting
Sovereign House,
Brentwood,
Essex. CM14 4SE.

Searcher
4 Whitmore Hill Cottages,
Whitmore Vale Road,
Grayshott,
Hindhead,
Surrey.

The Castle Inn
West Lulworth,
Dorset. Tel. West Lulworth 311

Ken Frampton
Wychwood Display Cases,
c/o, *Searcher* (Above)

Regton Ltd. (Garrett Agents)
82 Cliveland Street,
Birmingham. B19 3SN.
Tel. 021 359 2379.

Garrett Electronics, Inc.
2814 National Drive,
Garland, TX 75041
USA.

Appendix IV

Britain's national organisation charged with the duty of promoting, protecting and encouraging the responsible use of metal detectors, The National Council for Metal Detecting, has produced this eminently sensible Code of Practice:

1. Do not trespass. Ask permission before venturing on to any private land.

2. Respect the Country Code. Do not leave gates open when crossing fields, and do not damage crops or frighten animals.

3. Do not leave a mess. It is perfectly simple to extract a coin or other small object buried a few inches under the ground without digging a great hole. Use a sharpened trowel or knife to cut a neat flap (do not remove the plug of earth entirely from the ground), extract the object, replace the soil and grass carefully and even you will have difficulty in finding the spot again.

4. Help keep Britain tidy--and help yourself. Bottle tops, silver paper and tin cans are the last things you should throw away. You could well be digging them up again next year. Do yourself and the community a favour by taking the rusty iron and junk you find to the nearest litter bin.

5. If you discover any live ammunition or other lethal object such as an unexploded bomb or mine, do not touch it. Mark the site carefully and report the find to the local police and landowner.

6. Report all unusual historical finds to the landowner.

7. Familiarise yourself with the law relating to archaeological sites. Remember it is illegal for anyone to use a metal detector on a Scheduled Ancient Monument unless permission has been obtained from the Historic Buildings and Ancient Monuments Commission (English Heritage). Also, you should acquaint yourself with the practice of Treasure Trove.

8. Remember that when you are out with your metal detector you are an ambassador for our hobby. Do nothing that may give it a bad name.

9. Never miss an opportunity to show and explain your detector to anyone who asks about it. Be friendly. You could pick up some useful clues to another site. If you meet another detector user, introduce yourself. You may learn much about the hobby from each other.